GASTRIC BAND HYPNOSIS

RAPID WEIGHT LOSS FOR WOMEN

LEARN HOW
TO LOSE WEIGHT,
MAINTAIN HEALTHY HABITS
AND CONTROL
YOUR SUBCONSCIOUS MIND
THROUGH
HYPNOTIC VIRTUAL BAND TECHNIQUES

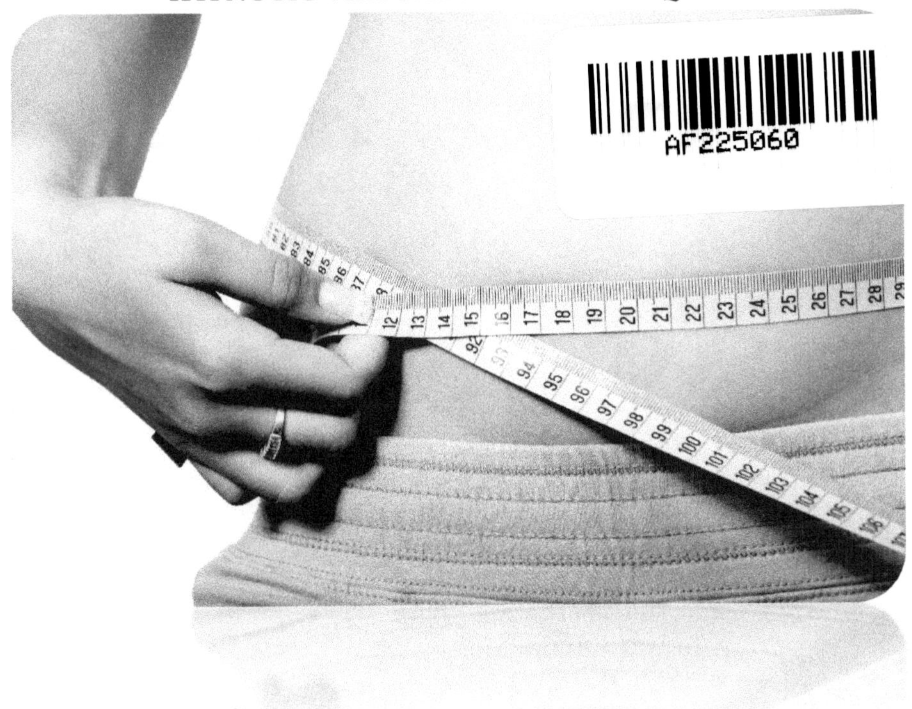

CAROLYN CONSTANCE

Additionally, the information in the following pages is intended only for informational purposes and should thus be thought of as universal.

As befitting its nature, it is presented without assurance regarding its prolonged validity or interim quality.

Trademarks that are mentioned are done without written consent and can in no way be considered an endorsement from the trademark holder.

TABLE OF CONTENT

Introduction

If you are trying to lose weight fast or just want to make sure that the weight is coming off as quickly and safely as possible, then it might be worth looking into gastric band hypnosis. This treatment may be a good option if you have tried other methods of weight loss but are not finding the results that you were hoping for. Gastric band hypnosis is also right for people who don't want to have stomach surgery in order to lose weight.

Gastric band hypnosis is a weight loss treatment in which a therapist will talk to you while you are in a state of deep relaxation. During this time, he or she will give you suggestions that will reprogram your subconscious mind. The goal of gastric band hypnosis is to make the patient feel full of fewer calories by changing the way that he or she thinks about food.

The average person who undergoes gastric band hypnosis loses around five pounds per month. Some people lose a lot more than this, and some lose less. The nice thing about gastric band hypnosis is that it allows a patient to have control over his or her weight loss. You can decide how quickly you want to lose weight and work with your therapist to make the process as safe and effective as possible.
In general, gastric band hypnosis is very safe. It does not involve any drugs or trauma to the body, and it will not damage any organs or result in any medical complications. There is also no need for surgery and no side effects are associated with getting this treatment.

Gastric band hypnosis is an option for people who have tried other forms of weight loss without success. It can also be a good choice if you don't want to have any type of surgery. However, gastric band hypnosis is not a perfect solution to every problem. For example, the start-up cost of this procedure may not be right for everyone. In addition, some patients may find that it works better for them than it works for their friends and family members.

Gastric band hypnosis is a good choice if you have tried other forms of weight loss and either found that they didn't work, or you didn't like the side effects. Gastric band hypnosis can also be a good fit if you do not want to have surgery and don't want to go through a lot of pain or torture in order to lose weight. However, gastric band hypnosis is not right for everyone since it might not work as well for some people as it does for others. Also, if you are interested in gastric band hypnosis, then make sure that your therapist has had the proper training and has used this treatment correctly.

When women start a healthy weight loss routine, they are bound to lose certain parts of their bodies faster than others. This is because of the different functions in men's and women's bodies and because of the difference in mass between men and women. Most often, a woman will lose weight faster from her midsection. This is what we also call belly fat or abdominal fat. Having a lot of this type of fat is not healthy because it is linked to diabetes, heart disease, and hypertension. Since women usually have more of this fat than men do, losing all or at least most of it will make them look and feel better.

However, the question now is: How can we accomplish that?

Studies show that gastric band hypnosis is a good way for women to lose belly fat and other types of excess weight around the body. This procedure was developed by Paul McKenna who was also known for his book I Can Make You Thin which has sold millions of copies in the UK. This treatment was designed to help women lose weight fast and all in a natural way.

This procedure can be used by both men and women, but it is more useful for women. Women have a lot of health problems, such as heart attacks, stroke, etc. This makes them vulnerable to medical complications which are not experienced by men. The chances of a woman having these diseases are higher than those of a man too. Hence the need to protect the heart and body when losing weight. It is for this reason that most hospitals have special units for obese females who need treatment from doctors specially equipped with handling these situations safely and effectively.

What Is Gastric Band Hypnosis?

Understanding the Hypnotic Gastric Band and how it Works

Gastric band hypnotherapy is a technique used to propose that you have a gastric band connected around your stomach to the intuitive to enable you to get more fit.

Gastric band medical procedure, thought about a final retreat, incorporates fitting a band around the upper segment of the stomach. This confines the amount of sustenance that you can expend physically, advancing weight reduction. It is an activity and, in this manner, involves future dangers and confusion.

Hypnotherapy of the gastric band or fitting a' virtual gastric band' doesn't include the medical procedure. Trance inducers utilize this technique to get the subliminal to think a gastric band has been fitted. The objective is to believe that you have had the physical activity on an oblivious level and that your stomach has diminished in size.

There is no medical procedure or medicine associated with the procedure, and it is thoroughly secure. In this segment, we will explore what is engaged with gastric band hypnotherapy, how it works, and on the off chance that it can work for you or not.

What is a Gastric Band?

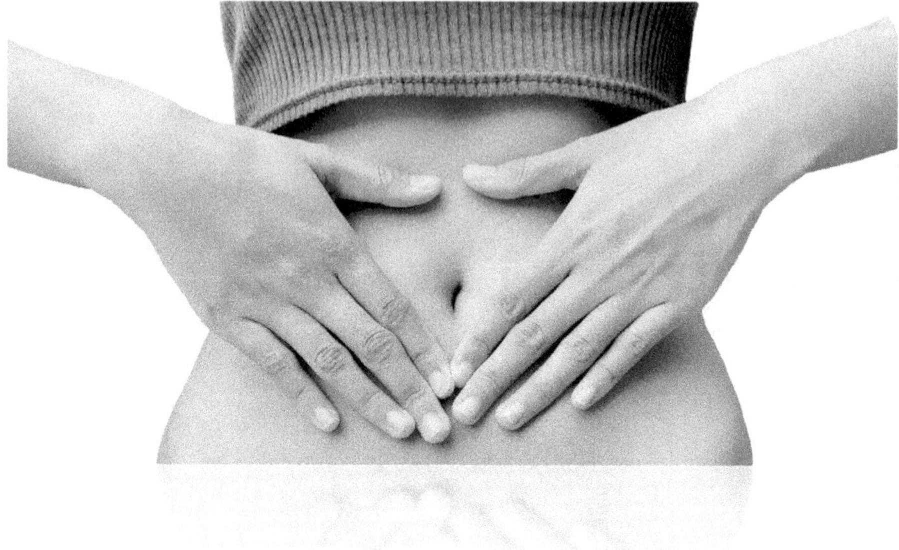

A stomach band is a silicone flexible apparatus utilized in weight reduction medical procedures. To create a modest pack over the gadget, the band is put around the upper part of the belly. This restrains the amount of sustenance that can be put away in the stomach area, making eating enormous amounts hard.

A gastric band will likely constrain the amount of sustenance that an individual can expend physically, making them feel full in the wake of eating next to no to advance weight reduction. It is a final hotel for most people who have this medical procedure after endeavoring for other weight reduction systems. Like any medical procedure, there are perils in fitting a gastric band.

Gastric Band Trance

Gastric band trance can be utilized without the perils that accompany medical procedures to help people get thinner. A two-dimensional procedure is utilized by numerous trance specialists. The first hope to characterize your enthusiastic eating's underlying driver.

Utilizing trance, the specialist can urge you to recall long-overlooked nourishment-related encounters that may now influence you subliminally. Before performing gastric band hypnotherapy, tending to and perceiving any unfortunate reasoning, examples concerning sustenance can be helpful.

Next, the trance specialist will play out the treatment of the virtual stomach band. The technique is proposed to recommend that you had an activity to embed a gastric band at a subliminal stage. The objective is to cause your body to respond to this proposition by making you feel quicker as though you were having a genuine medical procedure.

How it Functions

 How gastric band spellbinding works Using techniques for unwinding a trance specialist will get you a condition of trance. Your subliminal is progressively open to proposal in this casual state. Trance inducers are making proposals to your intuition at this stage. With hypnotherapy of the gastric band, this suggestion is that you have joined a physical band. The psyche is solid, so your conduct will change as needs be on the off chance that you are subliminal that acknowledges these proposals. More often than not, alongside the virtual gastric bands fitting's proposals will be created about trust and conduct to help you focus on this way of life move. Numerous specialists will likewise encourage strategies for self-mesmerizing so you can improve your activity after the session. It is likewise regularly prescribed to instruct yourself on nourishment and exercise to help physical wellbeing and prosperity.

The Process

Your first subliminal specialist session will likely be a unique counsel where you will talk about what you would like to get from hypnotherapy. This is an opportunity to talk about any past endeavors at weight reduction, eating rehearses, medical issues, and generally speaking nourishment frame of mind. This information will furnish the advisor with a clearer idea of what will help and whether to think about some other kinds of treatment.
The activity itself is expected to imitate the medical procedure of the gastric band to help your subliminal think it has happened. Numerous subliminal specialists will incorporate the sounds and scents of a working performance center to make the experience increasingly true. Your specialist will begin by carrying you to a condition of profound unwinding, otherwise called entrancing. You'll be aware of what's happening, and you'll generally be in order.
The specialist will address you through the system once you're sleep-inducing. They will explain bit by bit what is happening in a medical procedure, from being put under a sedative to making the primary entry point, fitting the band itself, and sewing the cut. A working auditorium's sounds and scents will improve the experience to persuade your inner mind that what is said is transpiring.

As expressed before, different proposals to improve self-assurance might be incorporated during the activity. Endless supply of the system, your trance inducer may show you a few strategies for self-spellbinding to help you stay at home on the track.

Some subliminal specialists will approach you to return for follow-up arrangements to screen the accomplishment of the virtual band and roll out any improvements. This happens when people additionally fit the physical band, proceeding with hypnotherapy sessions as a feature of long-term weight management, the board plan might be valuable for a few. This empowers the subliminal specialist to work with you to handle the hidden sustenance and confidence issues.

How am I going to feel afterward?

The general objective of the gastric band is to encourage a more beneficial nourishment association. If your subliminal thinks you have a gastric band fitted, your stomach will believe it's lower. This, thus, makes your mind send messages that, in the wake of devouring less nourishment, you are finished.

Perceiving when you are physically finished can be hard for the individuals who gorge. At times we eat only for taste (or comfort), overlooking whether we are physically ravenous or not. In developing smart dieting works on, figuring out how to perceive the physical vibes of being ravenous and being finished is helpful.

In contrast to gastric band medical procedures, there are no physical symptoms in the virtual gastric band. For a few, the real medical procedure may trigger the reflux of queasiness, regurgitating, and corrosive. Since mesmerizing, the gastric band is not a physical technique, it won't trigger such side effects.

The activity ought to be a charming and loosening up understanding, with most people revealing from entrancing an impression of quiet.

How To Get Convinced To Have A Physical Band Fitted

The best thing about the band is that it's totally different from other treatments, like liposuction or a tummy tuck. Unlike those kinds of surgeries, with the band, you can not only eat whatever you want (including pizza!). You also don't need downtime following your treatment since it's done using hypnosis. Hypnosis works on the mind and can help change habits without any discomfort or negative side effects.

Before you decide on having a band fitted, there are a few things you need to know about this kind of surgery. It is called Gastric Banding because it is done inside the stomach. It's not like liposuction where they remove fat from certain parts of your body. With the gastric band, it's all about restricting food intake before the body gets too full and starts storing energy in that part of your body rather than what you need it for. The gastric band surgery is purely cosmetic; the patient will still feel hungry: it's just that they won't feel as hungry as when they started with the band.

The procedure is called gastric band surgery or stomach stapling and uses saline to create an internal weight loss band. It will not work if you eat too much fat, so don't skip breakfast! The gastric band uses a balloon to keep it in place. This will stay there forever unless removed surgically.

It takes a little while for the treatment to work because you have to adjust your diet after the first week or so, but then it gradually reduces how full you feel. You can continue to have slimming surgery, get liposuction, or simply lose weight in other ways as well. After the gastric band is fitted, it does not influence other body parts as liposuction does. For example, if you want to have a chin slimmed down, liposuction is the way to go.

Although the procedure takes about an hour, you will need to go back for day surgery later on to insert the tube and drainage port. This surgery is scheduled for your second or third week after your initial band fitting.

How Does it Work?

The band creates a small pouch in the stomach that restricts how much food can enter and will then feel full faster than when you started with it. When you get hungry after having had a gastric band fitted, it's like feeling hungry when you are really full. If you stop eating, the band will eventually fall off within a few days. It can be removed by the doctor, but it is not advised to remove the band on your own.

The gastric band surgery or stomach stapling will not result in any new weight loss unless you manage to stay at your ideal weight for at least six months. If you lose more than ten pounds (5kg) during this period, then it's likely that you'll end up with a noticeable stomach bulge unless there are other factors involved like an upright posture. The gastric band surgery is completely safe and easy to perform.

The BPEGM procedure is used for patients who are obese or have been diagnosed with obesity-related diseases such as diabetes type II or hypertension (high blood pressure).

The patient is placed under anesthesia. After the anesthesia, a tube is inserted into the stomach and the band is fitted onto this tube. A port is then created in the small of the patient's back to allow excess liquid to drain from the stomach and after which time it can be removed.

The patient needs to drink at least 2 liters of water daily while drinking up to 6 liters (2 pints) per day for nausea relief. The band will not operate as an appetite suppressant for patients who are already taking medications that suppress appetite and/or who are already obese or have been diagnosed with obesity-related diseases such as diabetes type II or hypertension (high blood pressure).

How Much Does it Cost?

Many private health insurance companies may not cover gastric surgery (such as gastric band surgery) at all because of the way it works. You must either have private health insurance or pay out-of-pocket for your treatment. The cost ranges from $4,000 to $8,500 depending on your salary.
The costs may be covered by some healthcare insurance plans if the patient has been hospitalized for long-term treatment. If the surgery is performed within a hospital clinic instead of a hospital ward, the entire cost will be covered directly by the hospital or clinic.

Factors That Affect Your Aftercare

How much you weigh before surgery is one of the key factors that determine how quickly you will lose weight after gastric band surgery or stomach stapling. If you're 5-foot-5 and 154 pounds, then surgery will likely result in only a 10 percent weight loss per year. However, if you're 5-foot-11 and 240 pounds, a gastric band procedure can help you get rid of 15 to 30 percent of your body weight after six months.
If you've been diagnosed with diabetes or hypertension (high blood pressure), then your doctor may recommend gastric bypass surgery to help control these conditions. On the other hand, if you have pre-diabetes or obesity (body mass index is over 30), then your doctor may recommend gastric band surgery.
Patients who are severely obese (BMI is 40 or higher) could benefit from gastric bypass surgery. These procedures have been used since 1997 to treat extreme obesity (with or without pre-diabetes/type II diabetes). Gastric stapling may be used for stomach reduction in cases of severe obesity when banding proves unsuccessful.
However, gastric banding and other weight-loss surgeries are not a "quick fix" for losing weight quickly. These procedures can be complicated and dangerous if not performed by a highly-qualified surgeon in a completely sterile medical environment. The recovery process can take several weeks, and the patient will need to follow a strict diet and exercise program. Therefore patients should think twice before getting gastric banding surgery if they're looking for a quick fix. There is no better way to lose weight than the old-fashioned way – by eating healthy and exercising regularly!

How Powerful Is Our Subconscious?

Grace's naturally magnificent charm and beauty brought her a complete scholarship to a prestigious modeling college. She fell out after six weeks because her weight ballooned to more than two hundred pounds, which stayed for another fifteen years regardless of persistent weight reduction attempts. Jack, fifty years older, was overweight since high school, even though playing sports, doing regular exercise, also creating many efforts at weight reduction. Whenever his weight starts to fall, he feels fearful until he regains the pounds.

Mary has won and gained the same twenty-five pounds throughout her adult life. She knows the routine and activates; however, she feels so helpless to alter them and shed the pounds once and for everyone. Alex is a successful executive in a competitive tech industry that always struggles with his burden.

He works hard, makes a higher income, and will multitask better than many, but cannot restrain the size of the waist. Ted has been CEO of a global source firm. His friends saw him as he moved from being a photograph of wellness to some health hazard due to excessive weight reduction. Grace, Jack, Mary, Alex, along Ted, are actual cases we found in treatment for weight loss with hypnosis.

Like many other people, these folks once believed that food and eating were the issues causing their surplus fat. This chapter is all about what they discovered are the genuine culprit--the psychological mechanisms that affect or affect eating and weight reduction. We'll have a look at how inherent psychological problems are expressed in a way that triggers and keep excess fat. We'll learn more about using hypnosis to discover the use of feelings and burdens. We're not likely to speak about eating disorders--like bulimia, anorexia, and pica--or even other hurtful behaviors. This chapter is about the most common methods by which our bodies can gain weight and keep it on.

The Mind-Body Mirror

Considering these are out of our mind-body medication practice, let's briefly examine a few of the standard methods that physical ailments are created by the mind-body. There are various examples where suppressed and repressed emotions locate saying by manifesting as physical symptoms and ailments.

Emotions and psychological conflicts that Aren't consciously acknowledged, voiced, or Provided voice mayor will be voiced from the body. Here's a pervasive case. When anger isn't recognized and expressed, it can lead to muscles in your head, neck, and shoulders tightening up and stressed, which causes a pressure headache. It is the literal manifestation of something or somebody that's a pain in the throat. Another individual experiencing the very same feelings of anger may be burning over the circumstance, also expertise nausea, nausea, or an illness.

Your skin is the organ that's quite responsive to feelings. Also, a state of urticaria (hives) may erupt whenever somebody is getting under their skin or rubbing them the wrong manner or any time the individual is itching to say or do something, or even any emotion is erupting into the surface. Your emotions are emotions, such as happy, sad, or mad. If feelings or emotions aren't expressed, the mind-body will reflect them in imaginative ways.

Therapeutically, metaphors help us understand what the human body is expressing.

A figure of language or metaphor describing a psychological reaction like "a pain in the throat" is expressed through muscular strain and hassle, since the psychological frustration isn't being expressed differently. It can be a frequent encounter because, most times, it isn't okay or advisable to admit and convey anger or other emotions. For instance, if your boss embarrasses you or gets an unreasonable request, you can jeopardize your job if you have voiced your anger. Instead, you place it out of thoughts and go to another thing. Putting it from the mind doesn't place it from human anatomy.

Since you will notice from the hypnosis cases used in treatment, feelings and psychological conflicts could be placed out of thoughts, but not always from the body. You're able to suppress feelings or repress them. Suppressing feelings is if you intentionally decide not to consider them. Repressing emotions occurs whenever your subconscious does this without the advantage of choosing to perform it yourself. We'd love to spell out the difference between thoughts and feelings. Ideas are thoughts, beliefs, ideas, and conclusions on your own conscious or "thinking thoughts." Feelings or emotions are expressed in your entire body.
They arise in a crude place deep within the brain known as the limbic system. Both ideas and feelings are "items" in the meaning they're not only in your thoughts.

They involve power and chemistry, and they're transmitted and energetically throughout your nervous system along with other pathways inside the body. The chemical compounds called hormones, like dopamine, serotonin, noradrenaline, and acetylcholine, would be the common ones included.
If someone experiences mental sluggishness, then he can notice more psychological acuity if he comprises nuts, oatmeal, along with other choline-rich foods within his everyday decisions. Choline affirms the purposes of acetylcholine, which subsequently promotes memory and mental sharpness. We would like to highlight that these psychological and cognitive reactions and routines are real and happen to be analyzed for our purposes.

Feelings or emotions comprise pain, anxiety, guilt, despair, joy, anger, pleasure, bliss, contentment, serene, stress, and isolation. Notice that "poor" and "good" aren't from the record of feelings. Though we may say "I feel awful" or "I'm great," these aren't emotions. These are conclusions about what you believe; however, they aren't feelings. More correctly, if you create these announcements, you believe "I feel sick" or even "I feel well," which are approaches to explain how you're feeling, maybe not what you're feeling. Now, this is your only worth remembering: "Fat" isn't a feeling. Though folks say, "I feel fat," "fat" isn't a feeling.

Whenever someone says they're "feeling fat, then" it's a declaration about a feeling, like feeling fulfilled, filled, complete, or outside full. You could be thinking, "Why the big deal on the selection of words? I understand what I mean when I state that." The reason why we emphasize that is your feelings, as well as your voice about your emotions, are part of your own beliefs about yourself, and if you maintain these in understanding or talk them aloud, they're direct messages to your subconscious mind. Your mind-body finds all of it, and also long after it's from the mind (consciousness), it isn't from your own body's mind. You are going to want to select carefully what your goal will be to think and anticipate about your weight loss and exactly what and how you are feeling about it for it'll reflect it.

Saving Grace

One occurred to Grace that induced her to overlook her modelling college scholarship. She arrived at the office and expressed the desire to work with hypnosis to help her slim down. She clarified many different trials of weight loss methods that had been ineffective. Whenever she didn't lose fat, it'd return. She believed that there was "something" keeping her out of losing weight. In carrying her background, we discovered she had been thirty-six years older, married with three kids, ages eight, seven and five. Her weight was always over two hundred pounds for approximately fifteen decades. She grew up in the Midwest with a fantastic family and also had three sisters. Grace explained herself as the only woman in her household, having a weight issue. When asked regarding her weight record, she'd only say she "ate a lot." After finishing a thorough psychological and psychological evaluation, we proceeded to educate her about sculpting.

If she felt comfortable enough to move, we started with an induction method such as those on the sound with this publication. Grace relaxed readily into a trance country, wherein she had been absorbed in her thoughts and thoughts of a relaxing and enjoyable spectacle. As she pictured being on holiday with her loved ones, I provided hypnotic suggestions for her mind about letting her insight into the function or purpose of her extra body fat. In a couple of minutes, she seemed worried, and I asked her to explain what she was experiencing as she lasted. She explained riding a train and also becoming the very first to arrive in the modelling school. The government office has been shut; however, a friendly janitor assisted her suitcases and unlocked the door to her delegated dining space. She was getting tearful and stressed as she continued talking. I assured her she would disrupt the squint at any moment or she would move more gradually and professionally. I informed her that she understood she had been at our office today as she recalled something which happened afterward, fifteen decades back. Through her tears, she clarified the favorable janitor returning after that night, allowing himself to her chamber and hammering her.

The memory of the experience was rather exhausting and mentally draining for Grace. Discussing her following the trancework, I discovered it was nearly fifteen years since she'd thought about that adventure. She'd forgotten it. Initially, she opted to put this from her head, to curb this particular memory, but it had been put from her head so well that she'd forgotten that she forgot it. It had been repressed. She said this is the only real-time and location she had spoken to anybody about the encounter.

We spent a second session referring to her expertise in modelling faculty, and I requested her to earn some photos from this period. We used the photos to help her recall events so that she could chat about them at the security of treatment. She related that through the initial six months in school, her burden slowly improved, and she was anxious, fearful, embarrassed, depressed, and sleep-deprived. She didn't talk about the rape with anybody and moved home to wed her high school love.

He'd continuously accepted her for himself, and her burden was not a problem with him. Our counselling sessions demonstrated the goal of her excess body fat was a kind of defense. Her weight securely commanded her beauty so that she had been shielded from becoming the target of the following sexual assault. After she confessed, voiced, and revived the experience and feelings (fear, pity), Grace's weight loss plan was quite robust in cutting her dimension to wherever she felt joyful and secure. In her situation, we realize that the subconscious had been working out a role, and also there was a reason for the surplus weight.
It secured her and enabled her to feel secure. Though there was some time after she had been happy others found her appealing, the attack produced a panic that became linked to becoming captivating.

After analyzing these feelings and eliminating this anxiety, she had been free to discharge her additional weight and feel secure when she felt appealing.

Subconscious More Open To Suggestion During Hypnosis

If you are on a diet and have trouble sticking with it, there's help at hand. Hypnosis, one of the oldest ways of fighting obesity might just be the answer that you need. This article explains what hypnosis is and how it may help people to lose weight by giving them positive affirmations that they can listen to anytime they feel like slipping off their diet.

Hypnosis is one of the oldest ways to fight obesity - with good reason: this psychological therapy taps into your subconscious mind, where those feelings about overeating are stored.

As with dieting in general, rapid weight loss is not guaranteed with hypnosis, but it may be more effective for some people; furthermore, some lifestyle changes are advised to ensure that weight loss results become consistent.

Some research has shown hypnosis to be an effective form of weight loss. It has also been shown to be helpful for patients with conditions such as high blood pressure and stress-related illnesses. Theoretically, the body's responses to hypnosis could help reduce calorie intake by modifying appetite control mechanisms.

One study found that even if people were given a full night's sleep before weigh-ins, they still tended to put on the same amount of weight. It seems that the difference between being overweight and not is more about willpower than calories.

In the past, scientists believed that internal processes of your brain caused you to want to eat; it was not until recently that the idea of peripheral neural stimulation was introduced.

The most common type of hypnosis is focused on helping you eat less by making you more aware of your body's signals about hunger and fullness. Hypnotists also help you learn new behaviors and thought patterns that will make changes in your lifestyle easier to achieve.

Some research has shown that hypnosis is effective for weight loss, but there are not enough large-scale studies to determine exactly how much weight you can lose using hypnosis or how long it may take. Many people feel that they can control their eating habits, and if this is true for you, then you will probably be able to use the skills taught in hypnosis without any issues. However, if you have problems with food, then experts agree that proper help should be sought before beginning any form of rapid weight loss program. The biggest issue with rapid weight loss is getting enough nutrients; this is especially true in women because they need extra iron and calcium to avoid osteoporosis.

For some people, hypnosis can help them to overcome their fears associated with weight loss. As long as you are not afraid of letting go of the control you have over your eating habits, you are unlikely to have any problems.

This is supported by the fact that there is no medical evidence to support or comment on the effectiveness of hypnosis for rapid weight loss.

Preparation and training are essential when going through the hypnotic process; therefore, you may need a coach or therapist who can guide you through this as well as give suggestions throughout. For some patients, self-hypnosis may be enough; however, many people find that they need extra help from someone qualified to hypnotize them. A study published in the International Journal of Clinical and Experimental Hypnosis found that hypnosis is more successful for weight loss when it is done with a therapist than when you do it yourself.

Different Technique Of Gastric Band Therapy

Adjustable Gastric Band (AGB)

The Gastric Band Overview

The basic concept behind the gastric band is indeed very simple. The band functions like a tourniquet on the upper part of the stomach, limiting the amount of food you can eat. It can artificially divide the stomach into a small upper part and a much larger lower part. The bottom part can only receive food as soon as the strap allows.

The upper part quickly filled and it's slowly emptied. Limiting food intake will not cause any part of the stomach or digestive tract to be sutured, transferred, or rearranged. The fact that the band does not require rearrangement of the digestive system explains why AGB is currently the safest surgical option available for obesity management.

Controlling the amount of food that can be held in the stomach pouch is only part of AGB's promotion of weight loss. Perhaps the most significant impact of the band is its ability to minimize hunger. Anyone who has ever dieted knows that hunger is the main reason for failure. Only a small amount of food is needed to completely fill the space above the belt, but patients report that the feeling of satiety is the same as they have eaten for a big meal. After a meal, the food seems to remain in the upper segment for hours, resulting in a feeling of fullness.
In addition, patients with bands sometimes claim that they are not hungry, even if they eat nothing. The physiological reasons for this seemingly miraculous effect have not yet been fully grasped. However, any food or fluid inside the upper capsule appears to stimulate gastric nerve impulses or hormone release, thereby blocking the brain's starvation center.
Consequently, some individuals will not even feel hungry for a long period. The trick to allowing the band to work correctly is to establish a reasonable amount of constraints. When correctly balanced, the harness encourages weight loss while at the same time allows enough food and water to reach the rest of the digestive tract as well. Unless the strap is too loose it won't provide sufficient restriction to make it successful. When it is too close, the flow of food and fluid into the stomach can be severely blocked, leading to malnutrition and even extreme dehydration.
The space between the two sections of the stomach would be small, like an hourglass, if the strap is balanced properly. To achieve an appropriate

degree of restriction, the saline solution may be inflated by pouring it into a small storage tank, which is placed under the skin and connected to the belt by a tubing length. You can loosen the strap too by removing some or all of the saltwater. Though this sounds simple, it can be tricky and difficult to adjust the frequency band.

Surgical Placement of the AGB

Surgical Operation to put AGB is almost often performed using a procedure called surgical laparoscopy. Often this form of procedure is called minimally invasive procedure since there are no large incisions typical in conventional surgery.

Laparoscopy's advantages include reduced discomfort, faster healing, and less noticeable wounds. This is particularly important for obese patients because they are considered to have a higher surgical risk. Patients suffer less trauma, so they require fewer pain relievers. They heal faster, and can quickly restart regular activities.

During laparoscopic surgery, the skin and muscle walls insert a small tube called a cannula into the abdominal cavity. The cavity is then filled with carbon dioxide gas, similar to blowing a balloon. The gas pressure allows the surgeon space to operate between the internal organs and the abdominal wall.

A small telescope (called a laparoscope) is attached to a source of high-intensity light and a miniature camera. The camera is attached to a high-resolution video display, so it can provide the surgeon with an impressive view of the internal organs while placing the laparoscope into the abdomen.

The additional cannula is inserted into the wall of the abdomen and acts as a catheter for special devices used by doctors during surgery. On the video monitor, the surgeon and the whole team can watch every move.

Exposing the upper stomach area requires that the liver be physically lifted out of the stomach. The liver is normally large in extremely obese patients and somewhat well seated. This could prove to be the main obstacle to working close to the upper stomach. In serious situations, it is almost difficult to conduct the procedure safely on large "fatty liver." In preparation it is expected for the patient to have a low-fat, low-carb diet three weeks before surgery, to make the procedure safer and easier. This pre-operative diet can bring many benefits, as the liver usually shrinks sharply within a short period.

Preliminary dissection of the upper abdomen is performed prior to band placement during the operation. Experienced surgeons will typically perform this procedure in only a few minutes, although the process can take longer, depending on how much fat around the lower esophagus and upper stomach is present. In fact, men's physical problems are higher than women's. Obese males have more weight in the belly than obese women in other areas of the body, whereas obese women prefer to bear more weight

under the skin. When the drawstring is in the appropriate place, an upper
stomach bag will be produced which can only contain a few ounces of food.
AGB must be positioned properly around the stomach to be successful. If
placed too high, the bag will be too small to hold sufficient food and
provide sufficient nutrition. In fact, straps can be placed around the
esophagus which can cause problems, including swallowing difficulty,
blocked swallowing tubes, and even esophageal injuries.
If the strap is placed too low, then the bag is too large to lose weight
effectively. This makes bands insufficient to support weight loss for
patients. Additionally, heartburn is a common symptom if the band is too
low.
Two bands are most popular, mainly because they are the first two bands
on public sale, but as the band becomes popular, there will definitely be
many changes. The most popular one is 10 cm in circumference and can
hold approximately 4 cm3 of saline solution. Another popular band is 11
cm, which can hold 10 cubic centimeters of saltwater.
In most cases, the smaller size straps can be placed around the stomach
and surrounding fat without problems. However, if the stomach contains
too much fatty tissue, it can lead to early blockage, which means the band
is too tight and even liquid cannot pass through. This problem can be
avoided by removing some fat before placing the tape. However, removing
fat can be very difficult and there is a risk of a stomach injury. A better
option is to use a larger frequency band, which is specifically designed to
avoid the possibility of early blocking.
Once the appropriate size is selected, the surgeon first inflates it with saline
to ensure that it does not leak. It is then deflated and inserted into the
abdominal cavity through one of the cannulas. The surgeon passes an
instrument through the back of the stomach to pull the rubber band tube.
Then, pass the tube through the opening at the end of the strap and pull
gradually until the locking mechanism closes the strap around the
stomach. During this step, there is a risk of minor injuries to the stomach
or other organs in the area.
The surgical risk depends to a large extent on the amount of fat around the
stomach and the surgeon's laparoscopic experience. Since the surgeon
cannot really see the back there, it is difficult to find damage at the back
wall of the stomach. If a perforation occurs in this area, it may have
catastrophic consequences, especially if the perforation cannot be
identified immediately. Stomach contents spilling into the abdomen almost
always cause serious life-threatening infections. Fortunately, this situation
is not common in AGB compared to other procedures such as gastric
bypass surgery.
Esophageal Hiatal hernias are another possible complication during the
gastric band placement. This situation is actually very common and is often
related to heartburn. If a hiatal hernia is found, it should be repaired before
placing the strap. However, if the hernia is greater than one and a half
inches, the strap may not be an appropriate option. This condition is
related to a higher likelihood of problems after surgery, including band

displacement and possible hernia recurrence. For patients with heartburn, chest pain, or food reflux symptoms before surgery, it is best to perform some type of examination to rule out larger esophageal Hiatal hernias before deciding to use the band.

Putting a band on the stomach is a bit like putting a ring on a balloon filled with water. The stomach is a very flexible sac-like structure, and its shape will change dramatically over time. If the AGB is not fixed in some way, it may slide up or down as the stomach moves. In order to fix the strap in a position that needs to be retained, the surgeon pulls a portion of the stomach wall up above the strap and then sews it over the strap. The idea is to bind the strap in a tunnel formed by the stomach wall. The way the belt is fixed is almost the same as the way the belt loop fixes the belt. A small portion of the strap escaped the passage and began to slide upward, or more often downward. This is called belt slip.

Once the band is secured in place, one end of the tube is removed from the abdominal cavity through one of the cannula openings. Then, the pipe is penetrated under the skin and connected to a reservoir called "port". The port is made of hard plastic with titanium steel at the bottom. The front of the port is specially designed with a silicone rubber plug that can be pierced with a special needle that penetrates the skin. This allows the injection of saline solution to adjust the tightness of the band. After removing the specially designed needle, the silicon plug will be resealed. Normally, the port is located on the upper left side of the abdomen, but it can be located almost anywhere on the abdominal wall. It only needs a needle through the skin to access it. Once the port is in place, it will be covered with a layer of fat. The thicker the fat layer, the more difficult it is for the port to feel through the skin. For this reason, some surgeons choose to place the port on the sternum, where the fat layer is usually thin. Although this position makes the port easier to feel and access with a needle, the result may be visible swelling and swelling between the breasts. As the patient loses weight, this will become more apparent. Therefore, most surgeons tend to place the port on the side of the abdomen.

Once the port is sutured to the muscle, a soluble suture closes every small incision in the skin. Deck each incision site with a small dressing before the patient leaves the operating room. While this marks the conclusion of the treatment, for patients it's just the beginning: patients now have a new tool to help combat obesity.

Disadvantages Of Using A Physical Gastric Band

Doctor Alen Milgrom's gastric banding procedure involves a surgical procedure that minimally invades the stomach. This surgery used to be difficult but is now much easier and less drastic due to improved technology.

There are many advantages of using a gastric band for weight loss, but there are also disadvantages. Gastric bands have no side effects like medication that can cause nausea or constipation, nor do they affect the liver or kidneys like over-the-counter diet pills and supplements do. The surgery does have some risks of death if there is a complication during the operation, and complications can happen. Once the band is put in place, there are no more additional risks; however, the band needs to be monitored very closely by a doctor or nurse practitioner.

The gastric banding procedure cannot be reversed and patients that have this procedure must remain under their doctor's care for life. The advantage of this is that the weight loss can be slow and gradual.
The advantages of gastric banding over medication, diet pills, or supplements include: The gastric banding procedure does not disrupt your internal organs as medications do. Gastric bands can be removed if you

gain weight and want to lose it more naturally without surgery. (This only applies to the gastric band though not all gastric bands have this feature.) Gastric banding is a permanent solution to your weight loss problem. Expectations are that the patient's weight will gradually decrease to very low levels which means that the health risks and side effects from medications, diet pills, or supplements are not experienced.

There are disadvantages of using a gastric band, which is not necessarily true for other methods of weight loss. The procedure has a very high risk of complications because the duodenum (the part of the small intestine where digestion starts) is under direct tension from it being pulled into the stomach. There is a risk that the duodenum will be punctured during the procedure. Make sure that you schedule a consultation with your doctor or nurse practitioner before considering a gastric band surgery.
Beware of people who say that gastric banding has nothing to do with gastric bypass because they mean the same thing (a very large incision of the stomach and part of the intestine). The banding procedure is similar to adjustable gastric bands which are used in laparoscopic gastric bypass and use the same kind of "radiation therapy" as used in laparoscopic gallbladder removal (laparoscopic cholecystectomy) surgery, but also on some gallbladder removal surgeries. The banding uses the same kind of device as the gastric bypasses in many ways but it is performed through a much smaller opening and does not involve cutting up the stomach.
The procedure is done under sterile conditions, and no stitches are used in the stomach or intestines which reduces the risk of post-operative problems such as an infection. The bands are made of either solid silicone or coils, so over-the-counter medications can be used to treat symptoms like nausea that can occur with any surgery. Usually, one treatment lasts about six months and then another is given after a few weeks to remove weight. The procedure is not permanent because it can be reversed, but it cannot be removed unless the person gains weight again.
The safety and effectiveness of gastric banding have been proven through scientific studies. It has also been shown to result in a lower percentage of complications compared to other types of bariatric surgery such as gastric bypass (known as lap-band surgery). Gastric banding is considered an alternative to gastric bypass in that it offers a safe and effective way to lose weight that is less invasive than gastric bypass. However, there are still many risks associated with the procedure including death if complications happen during or after the procedure, long-term health issues, sensitivity to food, and even vomiting. Some people who undergo gastric banding may experience nausea and vomiting after the weight loss device is removed, though the number of these patients is very small.
The gastric band procedure requires that you be able to eat normally and have a full stomach so that you can put the device in place. You will be given medicine to help reduce nausea before your surgery. The anesthetics used during the procedure are not very strong but are still powerful enough to cause a short-term change in heart rate and blood pressure. There may

also be some bruising or swelling after the procedure, as well as discomfort or pain that occurs almost immediately after the band is put in place (which happens because of rapid weight loss). The band is removed when the weight loss has occurred and the patient feels full.

If you are diagnosed with morbid obesity, with a Body Mass Index (BMI) of 40 or greater, there is a great change in your life ahead of you. The baseline values for morbid obesity are from BMI 30 through 40. The good news is that if you manage to lose enough weight (20 to 50 pounds) through some other means, such as diet pills and supplements, most doctors will tell you that a gastric banding procedure can be performed at a later time. You will likely not need it earlier than ten years after your diagnosis because it involves putting a device in your stomach to regulate food intake for life. Gastric banding is not the final solution for everyone with morbid obesity, though. Many who are morbidly obese will need either gastric bypass or gastric sleeve procedures (also called gastroplasty) before they can safely undergo any operation such as a gastric band. Gastric bypass requires that a major part of the stomach be removed as well as the duodenum to make room for the new, smaller

stomach, while gastric sleeve surgery requires that only part of the small intestine be removed to reduce food intake by regulating how much is eaten at one time.

Many people who are morbidly obese consider gastric banding an option because it can be performed at a later date after other procedures have been done. Gastric banding is a relatively new procedure, and as such has not been around long enough to have a large number of studies completed yet. It is important to note that many studies have shown that this type of surgery does not improve weight loss much more than other types of weight loss procedures.

How Do Physical Gastric Bands Differ from Gastric Band Hypnosis?

Physical gastric bands are typically used for patients who are morbidly obese. The surgery is performed by making an incision in the stomach and then placing a belt around it. This forces the stomach to empty slower, which means that patients feel fuller faster, so they eat less. It also makes them more likely to chew their food properly and not gulp it down too quickly.

Weight loss with a physical gastric band is usually very slow, taking up to three years to be complete- if ever! However, this does make the weight loss permanent because the patient has changed their eating habits rather than just focusing on dieting with food restrictions or expensive meal replacements like shakes or drinks.

In contrast, gastric band hypnosis (GBH) involves hypnotizing the patient about 10-12 weeks before surgery. This helps them to become more relaxed and reach a deep level of hypnotic trance where they can feel and hear things that are taking place in their bodies without opening their eyes. In this way, they're able to accept the operation much easier than if they were just told what was going to happen and had no idea how it would really feel afterward.

Again, this makes the operation more permanent. The patient does not regain the lost weight easily (may have to do it for up to 10 years in this case) and there is no possibility of regaining it if they don't follow the operation's pre-occupations and dietary instructions.

The main message is that an individual will be able to lose more weight with physical gastric bands than with a procedure like gastric band hypnosis. GBH requires a lot of skill, so it will not be easy for most people to lose as much weight as they would have been able to with a simple physical gastric band.

An alternative to gastric band hypnosis is to do a combination of both procedures. The advantage of this would be to have a more permanent weight loss, but it does take a lot longer for the patient to reach a deep enough hypnotic state and achieve permanent weight loss than with an actual gastric band alone.

A patient is usually known by weighing themselves every day for the first month after surgery. Most patients will lose between 5-10% (about 10 kg) of their body weight within a month. This is because their bodies are still healing, and there's not enough food in the stomach to absorb. After three months, if they're losing around 1 kg a week, then it's likely that their body has accepted the operations and will not try to compensate by eating more. From here on, they can continue to lose weight at a rate of about 0.5-1 kg per week until their target weight has been achieved (this depends on individual personal circumstances). Researchers have found that patients who lose between 5-10% of their body weight as a result of physical gastric band surgery, are likely to keep it off for the rest of their lives. This is because the weight loss is permanent. After all, it's a change in eating habits rather than just dieting. This makes more sense than losing a huge amount of weight than trying to regain it, which is what happens with gastric band hypnosis.

In summary, physical gastric bands are effective and safe when used for patients who are morbidly obese. However, those who are not morbidly obese typically get much better results with gastric band hypnosis alone than they would if they were to have both procedures together.

Hypnotic Gastric Virtual Band

The virtual gastric band is a technique that combines hypnosis and subliminal reprogramming to make the stomach believe that it is smaller than it really is in order to reduce food intake and promote weight loss. This type of treatment is based on the belief that obesity is a permanent problem so the patient has to learn to eat a balanced diet voluntarily and effortlessly to avoid the problem of the rebound effect. Through hypnosis, the patient receives messages of healthy routines that he will put into practice after the session.

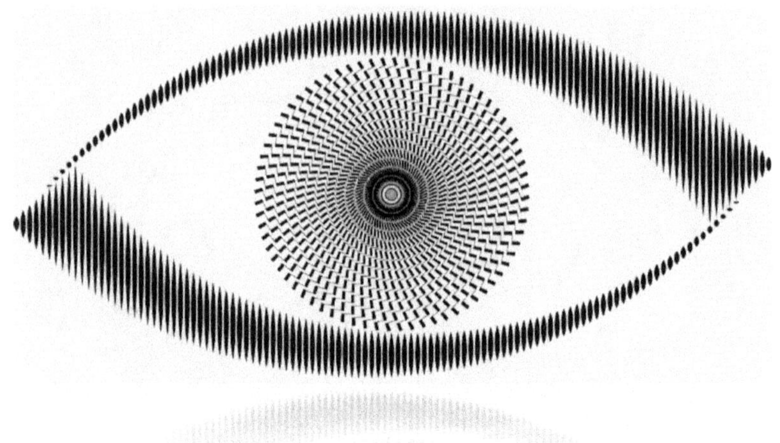

Virtual gastric band procedure

This technique acts similarly to those of stomach reduction, limits the amount of food ingested to lose weight. To get the feeling of satiety without using any external device, the patient must attend a hypnosis session. When the patient is in a state of semi-unconsciousness, he will receive subliminal messages to decrease the desire to eat and adopt new healthier eating routines.

This procedure is based on psychological techniques of cognitive-behavioral therapy (CBT) to change habits must be reinforced from time to time. The messages are losing strength over time, especially in long treatments. Besides, to receive recordings that the patient will hear periodically, he must attend other hypnosis sessions to adapt the messages according to the moment he is in.

This technique acts like other stomach reduction procedures such as the gastric band, hence its name. The patient will take less food as the stomach will send the satiety message to the brain before it is filled. The virtual gastric band can also be a complementary technique to other surgical treatments or not for stomach reduction, helping the patient to acquire the new routines without much effort.

Advantages and disadvantages

The main advantage offered by a virtual gastric band treatment is that there is no surgical intervention of any kind, it is a non-invasive treatment. Therefore, it does not require hospitalization, nor does it leave scars even if they are minimal.
Using a virtual gastric band treatment allows you to see results from the beginning. That is, the patient loses weight from the first week of treatment. This advantage favors the patient's self-esteem and strengthens the beliefs of the new routines.
In general, the cost of a virtual gastric band treatment is usually lower than that of other stomach reduction techniques.
However, virtual gastric band treatment is a relatively new technique for which there is not enough scientific evidence of long-term results.
In addition, it is necessary for the patient to have some implications because he must attend reinforcement sessions so that the subliminal messages do not lose strength. Weight gain in obese people is a long-term treatment.

Lose Weight with the Gastric Virtual Band

How many times have you considered losing weight? And how many others have you made a diet that you have abandoned because of the effort involved in getting rid of those extra pounds?
Have you ever raised that the causes are not only biological, that there must be psychological, emotional, or unconscious causes that make you continue to eat disproportionately or compulsively?
Ask yourself if you really want to lose weight and if so, we can propose a new, revolutionary and effective method, is the gastric virtual band with hypnosis.
A painless, risk-free, and easy method, as we provide it to you.

What is the virtual gastric band by the hypnosis method?

As you have read in the initial questions, and surely the answers have been many times referring to the first approach and concerning the second one, I am sure that you have also thought about it once but you do not find a

connection, that is, how you could imagine that it is not that you eat for eating, but you often eat for anxiety, for frustration, for disappointment, for boredom, for comforting you, etc....., in a nutshell: You eat your emotions.
It is at this last point that clinical hypnosis does its job since many behavior patterns, especially those related to food, are learned and automatic.
Through clinical hypnosis, we access the subconscious and create a series of suggestions to recreate an operation of a virtual gastric band that will allow the person to eat and notice satiety as if they had really operated on you, but without the side effects that may occur. Produce a real operation, since many people do not know how to physically identify the limit of their satiety.
Therefore, by implanting the gastric band through clinical hypnosis, the brain acts in the same way as if it were actually implanted since the mind believes it.
In the same way, we make a series of suggestions for each individual person to start eating naturally, without forcing anything, in a healthy and balanced way knowing when to stop and control for example when eating chocolate that does not eat all the box.
On the other hand and through another series of suggestions or hypnotic programming we make the person reduce or eliminate the desire that drives him to eat since normally the food he usually eats has many calories or sugar that later become fat and it is in extra kilos.
On the other hand, we create hypnotic suggestions to motivate people to move their body in any way, walking, exercising, but in such a way that these activities are carried out by people without that mental and physical effort that often involves them.
In some people, if necessary, we could find out through regressive clinical hypnosis if the causes of your overweight are related to some trauma or are the product of child behavior that you continue to perform as compensation or refuge from what is really affecting you and not solve.
In short, both through the implantation of the virtual gastric band by hypnosis and by issuing specific suggestions for each patient, we can get people to eliminate those kilos more definitively since at the end of the treatment we teach them a self-hypnosis technique so that they reinforce their new beliefs that emit so much with food, their figure thus achieving maintenance over time.

How Does Virtual Gastric Band Work

A virtual gastric band is presented as an alternative to diet slim. But how does it work? Each session consists of four sessions of 20 minutes each and follows four basic guidelines. The goal is to stop thinking about food all the time. It's simple in theory, but it can be a bit more difficult to do it logically. For simplicity, this method includes self-help advice, materials, and daily audio. In the second session, the stomach band is placed by hypnosis.

There is no type of surgery, but due to hypnosis (which does not cause pain or imply any health risks or side effects), the subconscious believes that the stomach has a stomach band and behaves as if it were smaller). Therefore, you can eat less, feel fuller faster, and lose the kilos you need to reach your ideal weight.

Remember that food is often used for anxiety, boredom, or indifference. In this way, you eat from hunger, not from stress. This means that virtual stomach bands and mental control will not only save you kilos but will also adopt healthier eating habits. One of the goals of a slim diet is to retrain your habits when you eat.
The virtual gastric band method is specifically designed for those who want to lose a few pounds more and are overweight or obese, but also for people who can no longer lose weight while on a diet, or when food is a substitute for anxiety. On the other hand, it is not recommended for eating disorders (anorexia or bulimia), diabetes, or irritable bowel syndrome.

Can A Virtual Gastric Band Really Have the Same Benefits Of A Physical One?

There are some very exciting advancements in the medical field these days, but as sure as there's a new technology available- there's also a new type of operation, procedure, or medication that seems to be making headlines. One surgery that has been gaining popularity is gastric banding; this article will explore what it is and whether or not you can achieve the same benefits with Hypnosis.

Gastric Banding is essentially an invention of modern medicine that functions as a tool for weight loss. A band is placed around the top of the stomach, restricting the amount of food that is able to pass into the small intestine enough to cause a person to reduce their caloric intake. This, in turn, causes weight loss.

Dieting and weight loss are definitely not easy tasks for most people. Fortunately, this is where Gastric Band Hypnosis comes in. A lot of people are curious about what it is and how it works but many find it difficult to understand or even considering stepping in. The same thing goes as far as Gastric Band Hypnosis- some people may want to know more but are afraid of trying it because they believe it may be dangerous or not work for them. It can be quite an interesting gxperience to try bit out, however, and many are very happy they decided to do so.

Gastric Band Hypnosis works with hypnosis and cognitive behavioral therapy. In a nutshell, it helps with making changes in your eating habits as well as other factors that are responsible for weight issues such as self-esteem, food issues, and stress.

It is important to note that a woman needs to be completely healthy before undergoing Gastric Band Hypnosis because they may choose to go through physical surgery after they complete the program. A trained therapist will help you make that decision and ensure you are completely prepared for whichever option you choose. One of the main benefits of Gastric Band Hypnosis is that it helps you shed weight without having to change your diet and lifestyle. Less than a month into the therapy, the Gastric Band Hypnosis will have worked, and you will be all set for physical surgery! Advanced hypnosis techniques are used to make the gastric band work and be effective. Hypnotists and hypnotic sessions have been effective in a wide range of medical practices, including pain control, smoking cessation, and weight loss surgery. Many people who have had gastric bands have found this to be a very positive experience and report that they were much happier with their results after going through the program than they were without it. The process of Gastric Band Hypnosis has many similarities to dieting and weight loss sessions you may find at a weight loss clinic or other medical facility but goes about things in a way that makes it more comfortable for both client and therapist alike.

The Gastric Band Hypnosis is given in a series of sessions with a trained therapist or hypnotist. A client can help to achieve specific goals regarding their weight loss and overall health, both physical and emotional. The most amazing thing about Gastric Band Hypnosis is that people report that they were able to change long-standing habits surrounding food and dieting with much more ease than they were able to before they undertook the program.

Women have reported that this type of therapy was spectacular for them, as it helped them achieve the weight loss results, they had been trying to accomplish for years without any success at all. Gastric Band Hypnosis also has the ability to help eliminate many of the issues that lead to other medical conditions.

The Gastric Band Hypnosis has been effective at controlling psychological stress and can be used successfully to treat a variety of issues, including symptoms such as panic attacks and phobias. Also, the Gastric Band Hypnosis can also provide relief from symptoms that are commonly associated with panic disorders and even those affecting the throat and voice box. For example, people who have had gastric bands report that they have been able to end their problems by talking continuously and experiencing bouts of hoarseness in their voices altogether.

One of the most helpful aspects of hypnosis is that it helps your mind and body to relax, thereby reducing many of the symptoms you may have considered to be normal. Hypnotic sessions are also known to help people relax their muscles and relieve pain during physical therapy.

As you can see, Gastric Band Hypnosis is effective at helping people achieve their goals even when other types of weight loss regimes have failed them before. Furthermore, it is a very safe therapy that has been used for decades and is regularly recommended with positive results.

Gastric Band Hypnotherapy can be particularly beneficial for women who may be carrying excess weight due to pregnancy. Hypnotic Gastric Band sessions are effective in helping women to lose the baby weight and change their lifestyle habits. The sessions are delivered discreetly at your own home. You will be guided step-by-step through the process and help to achieve your goals of losing weight quickly without the stress of dieting or starving yourself.

The Gastric Band Hypnotherapy is considered safe and secure, as it has a proven track record of being effective for women who are looking to shed the extra weight they have gained during pregnancy. You will be able to tap into your inner strength and emotions and feel more comfortable.

with yourself. You will also be able to access your mind through hypnosis and feel calm at times when you need it most.

Gastric Band Hypnotism is a process of deep relaxation that involves progressive muscle relaxation techniques that help you to go into a hypnotic trance, which can help you achieve the same results as those provided by surgery or medication. During the sessions, you will be able to visualize yourself healthy and thin. You will also be able to release many of the emotional problems that you have been experiencing for years. The Gastric Band Hypnotism sessions are easy to learn and can help improve how you feel about yourself on a daily basis.

The Gastric Band Hypnosis program, which was developed as a safe alternative to gastric band surgery, is now touted as being an effective way for obese people to lose weight without having surgery. Some people who are overweight may be considering having bariatric surgery and wish the process could be painless, but they do not have the time or finances for it. Gastric Band Hypnosis sessions are said to be able to assist people in overcoming this hurdle and achieving their weight loss goals.

Gastric Band Hypnotherapy is considered a safe and effective solution for people who wish to rid themselves of the problem of overeating. You will be free from the stresses that surround those who have had gastric surgery, or bariatric surgery, and you will feel confident and secure with your new dieting techniques. The hypnotist can help you get more creative with your eating habits so that you are able to lose weight without worrying about it too much.

Hypnosis is a process that helps to significantly improve your health, enhance your confidence and improve many aspects of your life. You will also be able to avoid any problems that may be associated with the use of the medical procedures that have been used for weight loss and loss management. With hypnosis you will be able to start winning, losing or maintaining a healthy weight. Hypnotizing yourself will also be beneficial because you will not be eating so much food that you cannot control yourself if it is taken away. This means that you will not get fat by overeating. You can also avoid feeling tired when you are trying to lose weight in order to achieve better results.

How to Find The Focus?

How to find the focus needed for gastric band hypnosis rapid weight loss for women?

1. Focus on yourself or those things that matter the most to you. Some people do not usually have a constant partner who will always be by their side during the ups and downs of their weight loss journey. If you are the type that does not have the support of a partner to encourage and motivate you, then this is good as long as it is not a problem for you. You can still focus all of your energy on reaching your goals.

2. Focus on your goals and be determined. This means that you should do your research and understand what it takes to achieve your goal effectively. Know what needs to be done first before turning to techniques such as gastric band hypnosis rapid weight loss for women. You should also set up a reasonable schedule and know how much time you will spend studying or working towards weight loss each day.

3. Do not quit if you fall behind in your weight loss journey at times. Everyone has his or her own challenges in life. Sometimes you will feel like

giving up as you see your weight not going down, but you should also remember to take it one day at a time.

4. Find the best support that you can get from friends and family. Surround yourself with people who believe that you can do it and who are willing to help motivate and encourage you when needed. Take advantage of them by asking for help when needed and accept their good intentions.

5. Get yourself a job that allows you to work from home if possible so that there will be fewer distractions for you while trying to lose weight.

6. Have the right attitude that will help you to reach your goal. Try not to be too stressed out when it comes to your weight loss journey. You should have a positive attitude that will help you focus and motivate you.

7. Eat healthy foods at regular intervals throughout the day so that you do not skip meals and go without eating meals completely. All of these things will positively affect your progress in losing weight even if there is a setback or fall off in progress sometimes every now and then.

What are some excuses for not losing weight effectively?

There are many reasons why people fail to lose weight effectively even with gastric band hypnosis rapid weight loss for women. Some of these include:
- Lack of motivation. It is okay if you do not always feel motivated to lose weight as long as you do not make an excuse to stop doing so. If you think that it is normal for you to be lazy, then this is not a good reason for giving up. You should stay focused and stick with the plan until it is fully achieved.
- Excuses about food. This means that you have the wrong attitude when it comes to food and how much should be eaten at any given time. You should always be aware of what foods to eat at what times especially during meals and snacks or when drinking sodas or juice during the day.
- Depression. If you are feeling depressed, you should allow yourself some time to work it out. Do not let depression make you give up on your weight loss plans. Try to find a way to escape the depression and move on with your life.
- Finishing off food or eating leftovers. You should only do so if there is no other choice, especially during parties or family gatherings. However, you should try to avoid this as much as possible and take leftovers home instead of finishing them off at the dinner table where they were originally served.

Can You Make It Without A Hypnotherapist?

Some people claim they can lose weight without a hypnotherapist. However, what they may not know is that it is not as effective without hypnosis. It might be best to find a hypnotherapist if you are looking to lose weight with gastric banding.

Practicing Self-Hypnosis for Weight Loss

Self-hypnosis or auto-hypnosis (as distinct from hetero-hypnosis) may be a kind, a process, or the results of a self-induced hypnotic state. Frequently, self-hypnosis is employed as an automobile to enhance the effectiveness of self-suggestion, and, in such cases, the topic "plays the twin function."

The nature of the auto-suggestive method maybe, "concentrative," in which "all attention is so totally focused thereon every little thing else is kept out of understanding." On the opposite, "inclusive," where subjects "allow all kind of ideas, emotions, memories, then on to wander into their consciousness."
Self-hypnosis or hypnotherapy is often a successful method of lowering anxiety and opening the mind to originalities or assumed processes, specifically when handling trouble practices like specific dependencies. Hypnotherapy may be a means of reprogramming how we believe.

We are stating that any quiet experience that takes you into a kicked-back or inspired frame of mind by assisting your real interest is de facto a hypnotic state, no matter what individuals might call it. By this interpretation, we will promptly see how television, P.R.P.R. firms, political publicity, religions, and advertising and marketing consistently utilize hypnotic procedures. It can, like all other powerful tools, be put to harmful use alongside the proper usage.

There is no enigma about just the way to utilize this device. It's that the majority of folks are denied the right to find out about exactly the way to use it for our very own good, while an equivalent "powers that be" are utilizing it to deceive, misinform, and regulate us. The reduced usage is also noticeable around us, so we'll specialize in the high uses, the particular application of the hypnotic procedure to supply recovery, health, and optimum performance. Doctors and psychotherapists widely utilize hypnosis to treat physical, emotional, psychological, and behavioral disorders. In maintaining with this healing use these tools, Dr. Miller has developed this meaning:

Hypnosis may be a procedure employing a particular collection of tools also as skills that:

Allow a private to maneuver in and out of various states of consciousness. Make it possible for the customer to help in understanding (the aware mind). Are utilized to enhance or reduce particular patterns of thinking, sensation, behaving, thinking, or relating. This way may influence the body's cells, the spirit, the thoughts also as photos in mind, and the assumption system. Appropriately utilized, it can help with healing and even integrity at every degree of order.

Is Self-Hypnosis Weight Loss Right For You?

Self-hypnosis is an efficient approach for ladies to reduce in exceptional circumstances. There'll be a spread of questions when determining if this strategy will be used for weight loss. Who can I trust, how long will it take, hypnotics alone will do the trick? While many promoters of audio and videotapes represent rapid self-hypnosis weight loss, it's essential to differentiate between those that offer a broader weight loss regime and not simply believe self-hypnosis as a moment healing procedure. Research by Vanderbilt University criticized most self-hypnosis weight loss methods on the internet; however, it found that some pages offered what seemed to be legitimate self-hypnosis weight loss programs.

Here we offer you valuable knowledge to make informed decisions on whether you employ self-hypnosis as to how to attenuate your weight or whether diets and medicines haven't worked for you, or whether you discover self-hypnosis as your primary plan to reduce. The great news is that weight loss through self-hypnosis is usually considered safe if someone qualified for training in these techniques has appropriately trained and advised you. Besides, the value of this sort of weight loss is generally less than many other choices if you do not need a different technique to realize your objective in your particular case. Nonetheless, most people may have additional strategies, such as exercise and nutritional therapy. If you would like a quick fix, other options are available, but they're far more expensive, including loss of weight of Bariatric.

A variety of organizations provide clinical monitoring and credential requirements that help uphold hypnotherapy standards and ethics. The American Council of Hypnotherapy Examiners can also be the group mostly dedicated to certifying hypnotherapy colleges. Another association, founded by the National Board of Certified Clinical Hypnotherapists in the 1990s, created a certification framework for practitioners to line up guidelines for the hypnosis field. The National Council for Licensed Clinical Therapists defines itself as 'an educational, scientific and professional hypnotherapist organization which promotes public and professional knowledge of the advantages of hypnotherapy and supports research project into the uses of hypnotherapy.'

While the hypnosis practitioner is significantly confirmed, it's not always foolish evidence or the sole deciding factor when it involves self-hypnosis. As in the medical field, doctors aren't certified by the board in their specific medical sector but are non-incompetent and may serve their patients well. It's advisable to see any reports or references that require independent verification of the practitioner's talents.

Consider claims that appear too good to be accurate and whether other options could also be more suitable for you, counting on your circumstances, like bariatric weight loss, which we offer with further information as an alternate self-hypnosis weight loss.

Self-Hypnosis Helps PCOS Weight Loss Efforts In Women

Most PCOS women can solve much of their health issues by losing only 7% to 10% of their weight. Nevertheless, the metabolic nature of PCOS can cause a loss of weight. Some studies indicate that ladies with PCOS need to work 25 percent harder than lean women to use an equivalent amount of stored fat as energy. Home self-hypnosis is a required method that ladies with PCOS may use to realize significant weight loss.

Self-hypnosis may be a way to rapidly and effectively understand new behaviors. Weight loss and, above all, keeping it off involves developing new behaviors. Self-hypnosis may be a healthy and fun way to improve your learning. It allows you to ascertain immediate outcomes, which increases your interest in learning more. It seems that what you spend some time doing features a substantial effect on what you do and what you do. What you expect would have tons of impact on what you encounter. Ninety percent of individuals losing weight recover, plus more-the numbers are well-known to dietary people for all times and are expected folks, ninety percent. Once you are willing to reduce (again and again), encouraging your efforts in self-hypnosis could also be the key to lifelong success.

There is a gaggle of individuals who lose substantial weight and never recover. 10% are people that have learned the way to sustain a considerable loss of weight for years. They share other characteristics:

They're all eating but fat;

They all practice regularly, and most days average an hour of activity.

They all keep an in-depth eye on the scales and check the reality regularly.

Hypnosis, or, significantly, self-hypnotization, can help you find out this behavior and ENJOY. The primary two actions show the sense 'just eat well and exercise,' which frustrated millions who regularly try not to do that. The third item, the daily scale-checking fact, suggests the key to breaking a cycle of failure the plagues most dietitians.

Careful people learn to attach the dots. "If I do so, I buy similar results; I buy different results once I do so." Keeping an in-depth eye on your bathroom scale, as you reduce and particularly once you move to a healthier lifelong diet, will improve the insight you've about what behaviors are becoming your results. Health research explores how our perceptions and attitudes are formed. "To research cognition is vital the notion that beliefs are often distorted with expectations," said Michael I. Posner, an emeritus neuroscience professor at the University of Oregon and a specialist in attention. "But we get to the processes now."

Hypnosis may be a method of deep relaxation that significantly increases the power to think. It's a strong and potentially misuse operation. On the opposite hand, self-hypnosis may be an excellent device that you manage for your own best interests.

The recent studies of hypnosis-prone people's brain activity indicate that their brains have significant improvements in the way they interpret knowledge as they act on suggestions during Hypnosis. The changes fundamentally change how people see, feel, hear, taste, and interact with what's real. Hypnosis can alter the perception of the truth of a private. So, standing on the size and searching out for 150 pounds and thinking, "I'm fat!" you teach yourself, and you believe that you're a fat man. Seeing the 150 on your scale and thinking, "I am an individual losing fat," you're more likely to feel this (especially once you saw 154 every week ago) and to behave sort of a one that loses weight. And then, that is what you do.

Hypnosis was well-known for dubious entertainment. A hypnotizer allows a participant to trance or relax and implies that a hypnotized person may clarify reality. Once you say that you are like a chicken – if you can click on the stage at any point, you'll entertain the audience with chicken behaviors. The suggestion that you simply do so accidentally is in dispute. There's no proof that a hypnotized person behaves in ways that contradict his or her beliefs or will. But if you're able to be an entertainer (take a stage, as any unhypnotized volunteer does), then you will be ready to click once, if this is often the entertainment you suggest.

Although it does little work, Hypnosis has been utilized in medicine since the 1950s to treat pain and treat anxiety, depression, trauma, irritable bowel syndrome, and food disorders. Throughout India, physicians used Hypnosis effectively as anesthesia also for limb amputation in the 19th century. Hypnosis was not used until ether became available.

Brain experts also do not precisely know what the hypnotic state is. This fact might just be a traditional sort of deep focus in which you avoid stimuli in the room while concentrating on your thoughts. Recent work on Hypnosis and feedback also offers new insight into the brain's training process and everyday functioning, consistent with Dr. Posner.

It shows that information from the eyes, ears, and body is transferred to the brain's primary sensory areas. This way travels from there to other places where understanding takes place. For instance, a light-weight that bounces off a rose first enters the attention and becomes a pattern that's sent into the visual center of the brain. There's an appreciation of the rough sort of the rose. This pattern is then sent to the following functional area, where color is defined, then to the next place, where the shape and color are added to make the rose image, alongside the other rose information you simply have gathered.

They view sounds, fragrances, touches, and other sensory details in the same way. This direction of flow is named feedforward by researchers. As basic sensory information is converted to a comforting feeling in bundles of nerve fibers, the info is transported from the bottom upward.

The surprise is that the amount of traffic that's called feedback from top to bottom. There are ten times as many nerve fibers that carry information as they carry it up.

What Is Self-Hypnosis?

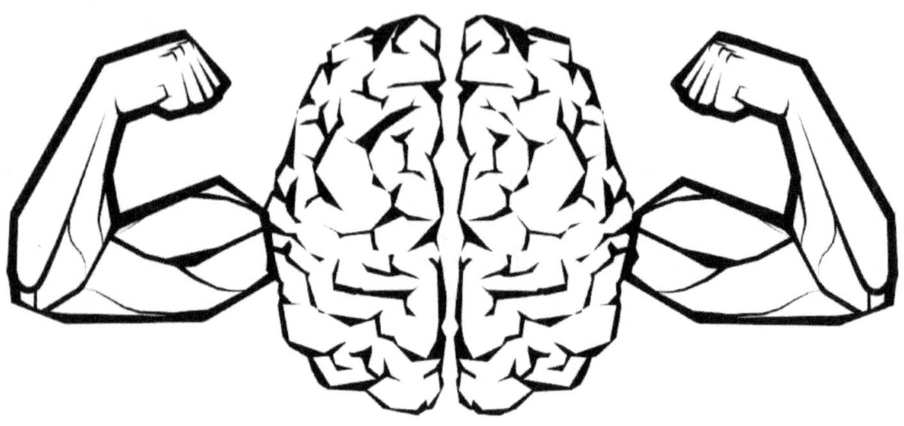

Self-hypnosis is a powerful method in which you talk right to the subconscious mind or part of your brain. It gives you a way to eliminate any obstacles and confusion within the dialogue of your mind-body. Self-hypnosis is still considered a mystical phenomenon by many people, even though this technique can be seen as prayer. You are alone, and you concentrate on your well-being. If you like, you ask God or a supreme being you believe in to help you. This practice also includes meditation (just like praying does), as well as chanting, mantras, inner confirmation, or affirmation. When you have to perform at work or college, you make such statements like "I don't fear; I'm fine"; "I can do it" or exactly the opposite, like "I can't do it. Everybody is better than me," etc. Even when we imagine ourselves in a different scenario from what is currently happening, we are programming ourselves. What you are doing is continuously hypnotizing yourself. Self-hypnosis helps us to come into contact with the unconscious through the use of a specific language, aimed at awakening some parts of ourselves by leveraging archetypal symbols. Self-hypnotization is self-programming. Our unconscious understands the symbolic messages of words rather than their rational meaning; that's why figurative language is used in hypnosis for inducing the individual to relax and to focus on the inner world. We are embedding a vivid, information-rich image with emotions in the subconscious mind.

However, we must learn to pray, or let's say hypnotize ourselves accurately! Self-hypnosis is the ability to apply techniques and procedures alone to stimulate the unconscious to become our ally and involve it directly in the realization of our goals. By learning the essential elements of communication with the unconscious mind, it is possible to become able to reprogram activities of our unconscious. Self-hypnosis is a method that does not dismiss the support of a professional but has the advantage of being able to be performed independently. This is possible through the use of CDs and DIY courses made by hypnotists to make this practice accessible to a larger number of people with significant advantages, even from an economic point of view!

It is merely a process of moving variables; you become the inductee of the relaxed state and the one who suggests the positive ideas for change on yourself. You are both the guide into the relaxed state and the one experiencing the relaxed state. While this might seem like it ups the ante and makes the process much more complicated just by increasing your number of roles and responsibilities, it is much simpler than you could ever imagine.

What is Self-Hypnosis For?

It was Milton H. Erickson, founder of modern hypnotherapy, who gave an exhaustive illustration of the effects and purposes of hypnosis and self-hypnosis. The scholar stated that this practice aims to communicate with the subconscious of the subjects through the use of metaphors and stories full of symbolic meanings (Tyrrell, 2014).

If incorrectly applied, self-hypnosis can certainly not harm, but it may not be useful in attaining the desired results, with the risk of not feeling motivated to continue a constructive relationship with the unconscious. However, to do it as efficiently as possible, we need to be in a relaxed state of mind. So, accordingly, we start with relaxation to gather the attention inside, while suspending conscious control. Then we insert suggestions and affirmations to the unconscious mind. At the end of the time allocated for the process, a gradual awakening procedure facilitates the return to the state of permanent consciousness. When you are calm, your subconscious is 20-25% more programmable than when you are agitated. Also, it effectively relieves stress (you can repair a lot of information and stimuli you understand), aids regeneration, energizes, triggers positive physiological changes, improves concentration, helps you find solutions, and helps you make the right decisions. If the state of conscious trance is reached, then if the patient manages to let himself go by concentrating on the words of the hypnotist, progressively forgetting the external stimuli, the physiological parameters undergo considerable variations. The confirmation comes from science, and in fact, it was found that during hypnosis, the left hemisphere, the rational one, decreases its activity in favor of the more creative hemisphere, the right one (Harris, n. d.).

You can do self-hypnosis in faster and more immediate ways, even during the course of the various daily activities after you have experienced what state you need to reach during hypnosis.

A better understanding of communication with the unconscious mind highlights how indispensable our collaboration is to slip into the state outside the ordinary consciousness. In other words, we enter an altered state of consciousness because we want it, and every form of hypnosis, even if induced by someone else, is always self-hypnosis.

We wish to access the extraordinary power of unconscious creativity; for this, we understand that it is necessary to put aside for a while the control of the rational mind and let ourselves slip entirely into relaxation and into the magical world of the unconscious where everything is possible. Immense benefits can be obtained from a relationship that becomes natural and habitual with one's own unconscious. Self-hypnosis favors the emergence of constructive responses from our being, can allow us to know ourselves better, helps us to be more aware of our potential, and more able to express them and use them to foster our success in every field of possible application.

How Self-Hypnosis Works?

We all want time to just relax, dream, pretend. It refreshes the physical body and rejuvenates the spirit. It gives us just that when we practice our hypnosis: a very personal moment to enliven and be able to enrich our mind and body. The procedure is literally over. You need nothing more than a secure and comfortable venue.

Simple Rules

There are certain guidelines for hypnosis, and they make sure the practice is the most effective and has the greatest advantages. Find a convenient and quiet spot in your home or office when you're ready to start using the audio, where you can sit in a chair, recline or even lie down. Make sure you're comfortable, and you don't have to pay attention to anything else in a spot. Do not listen to your work on trance while driving a car or running some form of machinery. In order to practice your self-hypnosis properly, it is helpful to agree on a daily time each day or night. Bedtime is a perfect opportunity to enjoy your job in a trance, and training at this time can be a wonderful way to reach a restful sleep.

Distractions and interruptions are possible. Using them instead of making them torment you and drive you away from your job in a trance. To enhance your experience of trance, use the sounds in the environment around you. For example, you might hear a sound while doing your hypnosis, and start thinking that this sound distracts you. You then concentrate more on the diversion than on your hypnosis. You may be tempted to fight it — which takes energy off the hypnosis. Instead, when you notice a sound that appears distracting or annoying at first, take control of it by giving it your permission as a background sound to be here, giving it a task, for example by saying that "the barking dog's sound makes me go deeper and deeper inside" or "the fan motor sounds like a waterfall that's a soothing background tone." In our private practice in Tucson, there's a day school that always lets the kids play during one of our hypnosis sessions. That is when we say, "Children's sound can be a background sound that helps you to go deeper and deeper into yourself now." This is part of our philosophy of "using all."

Distractions also include the feelings you can feel in yourself. You may find yourself feeling, for example, a part of your body that itches. The more you focus on itching, or scratching the itch, the less you concentrate on the trance.

You are just reminding yourself at those times that you have permission to move your attention back to your trance or daydream and let the itch go unravel. We teach patients a similar way of focusing attention away from the "distraction" of pain when working with them. If you have trouble letting go of an annoying distraction, you may need to order it to be there as a background sound or feeling, allowing you to go inside more comfortably. Detach yourself from anything your commitment to your hypnosis is competing with. Let go of any dispute with the world. Just let it be there and you won't notice it again sooner or later. Once you learn to accept a feeling, a noise, or another factor that interferes with your hypnosis, you don't let it affect you any longer.

The Law of reversed effect

There is a law in hypnosis, called the Reversed Effect Law, which says that the more you sometimes try to do something, the more it doesn't happen. An example is when you want to say a name that you think you know—it may be a title to a book, a person, a movie—but at that moment you can't say it, and the more you try, the less it is there. The name comes when you say "I will remember later" or "It will come to me later," to your subconscious mind. By letting go of the question "What is the name? What name is it? "You activated your subconscious mind to get the answer right now, and it always does. So, the Reversed Effect Rule is that it just gives you the opposite (the reverse) when you are working too hard for it.

Simple procedures

Becoming absorbed in your thoughts and ideas is that gentle journey into the center of yourself called "going into a trance." Simple self-hypnosis techniques include going into a trance, deepening the trance, using that state of trance to give the mind-body messages and suggestions, and coming out of trance.

How To Identify The Root Cause Of Your Emotional Eating

Whether You're pleased with your body fat or not, it's what it is, accept your present weight is a direct outcome of your lifestyle habits, namely the quantity and kind of food and beverage you like and your routine exercise habits and activity levels. A whole lot of bad eating habits are due to emotional eating; this is if our ingestion is ordered by how we're feeling, and we work with food to help us feel better. This is also referred to as relaxation eating, and generally entails excessive snacking or binging fatty foods that are fatty.

Emotional eating is a massive problem for a lot of men and women who struggle with their weight and typically highlight a poor men relationship with food. You may just break the custom of emotional eating should you determine what causes one to bite in this fashion; you need to discover the feelings and situations that cause you to lose control of your eating habits. Eating for comfort to cheer up yourself can develop into a vicious circle since you are able to become more miserable as you pile weight, forcing you to flip into food and make things worse (so it goes).

Here are a number of the usual triggers that could let you eat too much on a normal basis:

- Stress.
- Inadequate self-esteem.
- Depression.
- Boredom.
- Loneliness.
- Unhappy with your own body form.
- Marital or relationship problems.
- Financial worries.
- Deficiency of energy and inactivity.
- Greed.

People Rarely meet their emotional needs with a fresh green salad or even excessive quantities of fruit. Emotional eating normally involves consuming copious quantities of crap and convenience foods and candy snacks like chocolate and cake. Let's examine a few strategies that can help you manage your relationship with food and prevent you from binge eating.

Stress

Ever see how stress causes you to be hungry? It is not only on your mind. If stress is chronic, as it so often is in our hectic, rapid universe, your body generates elevated levels of the stress hormone, cortisol. The more rampant stress in your lifetime, the more inclined you should turn into food for emotional relief.

Stuffing emotions

Eating is a method to Silence temporarily or "things down" uncomfortable emotions, such as anger, anxiety, despair, anxiety, loneliness, bitterness, and shame. As you're numbing yourself with meals, you can prevent the difficult emotions you would rather not believe.

Boredom or feelings of emptiness

Do you eat just to give Yourself something to do, to alleviate boredom, or as a means to fulfill a void in your life? You truly feel unfulfilled and empty, and meals are a way to occupy your mouth and your own time. At the present time, it fills you up and distracts you from inherent feelings of purposelessness and dissatisfaction with your life.

Childhood customs

Think back to your own youth Memories of meals. Can your parents reward good behavior with ice cream, just take you out for pizza once you have a fantastic report card, or even give you candies if you're feeling unhappy? These customs may often carry over into adulthood. Or your ingestion might be driven by nostalgia--for precious memories of grilling hamburgers in the backyard with your father or drinking and baking snacks with your mother.

Childhood growth

For many people, emotional eating is A learned behavior. Throughout childhood, their parents provide them snacks to help them cope with a challenging day or scenario, or as a reward for something great. As time passes, the kid who reaches a cookie following a bad grade on evaluation might grow to be a grownup who catches a box of biscuits after a demanding day on the job. For instance, like this, the roots of emotional eating are heavy, which may cause breaking the habit incredibly challenging. Sometimes, people may eat so as to adapt; for instance, people could be told "you've got to complete your plate," and also, the person may eat beyond the point where they feel fulfilled.

Social influences

Getting along with other Men and Women To get a feast is a decent method to ease stress, yet it could likewise prompt indulging. It's anything but difficult to enjoy on the grounds that the food is there or essentially in light of the fact that every other person is eating. You could likewise gorge on social circumstances from nervousness. Or then again perhaps your family or friend network spurs you to gorge, and it is significantly simpler to go all together.

Negative impact

Negative affectivity is a character quality including negative feelings and insufficient self-idea. Negative feelings experienced in negative impacts contain outrage, blame, and tension. It's been found that specific unfriendly effect guideline scales called enthusiastic eating. An inability to pronounce and recognize the emotions made the person feel inadequate at controlling negative impact and thus more inclined to participate in emotional eating as a way for coping with these negative emotions. Further scientific research concerning the relationship between negative affect and ingestion uncover that, after undergoing a stressful event, food intake is associated with decreased feelings of adverse effect (i.e., Feeling awful) for individuals enduring high levels of chronic stress. This relationship between feeling and eating better indicates a self-reinforcing hierarchical pattern involving elevated levels of chronic stress and the consumption of highly palatable foods as a working mechanism. Contrarily, research conducted by Spoor et al. Discovered that negative affect isn't significantly linked to emotional eating, but both are associated through emotion-focused coping and avoidance-distraction behaviors. Though the scientific consequences differed somewhat, they suggest that adverse influence does play a part in emotional eating. However, it might be accounted for by other factors.

Connected Ailments

Emotional eating as a Way to deal Might be a precursor to developing eating disorders like binge eating or bulimia nervosa. The relationship between emotional eating as well as other ailments is large because of how emotional eating and those ailments share key attributes. All the more explicitly, they're similarly connected with feeling-centered adapting, maladaptive adapting systems, alongside a ground-breaking antipathy for negative feelings and incitement. It's very important to say that the causal management hasn't been established, meaning that although emotional eating is thought to be a precursor to those eating disorders, in addition, it might be the result of those ailments. The last hypothesis wherein enthusiastic eating occurs in response to some other eating malady is upheld by research, which has uncovered passionate eating to be basic among individuals previously experiencing bulimia nervosa.

Biological And environmental variables

Stress impacts food tastes. Quite a few research -- given, many of these in creatures have demonstrated that physical or emotional distress raises the consumption of food high in sugar, fat, or even in the absence of metabolic shortages. Once ingested, fat- and - sugar-filled foods appear to get a feedback effect that combats stress-associated reactions and emotions since these foods activate dopamine and opioid releases, which protect from the unwanted effects of stress. These foods actually are "comfort" foods because they appear to counteract stress, but rat studies reveal that occasional access to consumption of those highly palatable foods generates symptoms that resemble opioid withdrawal, implying that high fat and high-sugar foods may get neurologically addictive a couple of examples in the American diet could include: burgers, pizza, French fries, sausages, and salty pastries. The most typical food tastes are in decreasing order from candies energy-dense meals, non-sweet energy-dense food afterward, vegetables, and fruits. This may bring about people's stress-induced craving for all those foods.

The stress reaction is a Highly-individualized response, and individual differences in physiological reactivity can also result in the evolution of emotional eating customs. Girls are somewhat more prone than men to resort to eating as a coping mechanism for stress, as are overweight people and people with histories of dietary restraint. In 1 study, girls were subjected to an hour-long social stressor activity or even a neutral control condition. The women were subjected to every condition on various days. Following the actions, the girls were invited to a buffet with healthy and unhealthy snacks. People who had elevated chronic stress rates and very low cortisol reactivity to the intense stress task consumed more calories out of chocolate cake compared to women with reduced chronic stress levels following both control and stress conditions. High cortisol levels, together with higher sugar levels, might be accountable for stress-induced ingestion, as research suggests high cortisol reactivity is associated with hyperphagia, an abnormally enhanced desire for meals, during stress. Additionally, because glucocorticoids trigger hunger and especially increase one's desire for high fat and high-sugar foods, those whose adrenal glands normally exude larger amounts of glucocorticoids in reaction to a stressor are somewhat more likely toward hyperphagia. Furthermore, people whose bodies need more time to clean the blood of excess glucocorticoids are likewise predisposed.

These biological variables can Interact with environmental components to additionally activate hyperphagia. Regular intermittent stressors activate recurrent, irregular releases of glucocorticoids in periods too short to permit a comprehensive return to baseline levels, resulting in elevated and sustained levels of desire. Thus, those whose lifestyles or professions involve regular intermittent stressors over extended intervals thus have a higher biological incentive to come up with routines of emotional eating, which places them at risk for long-term undesirable health effects like weight reduction or cardiovascular disease.

The rationale is supporting stressful Ingestion: (1) emotional charge of food selection, (2) emotional reduction of food consumption, (3) impairment of cognitive consumption controllers, (4) ingestion to modulate emotions, and (5) emotion-congruent modulation of ingestion. These are split into subgroups of Dealing, reward improvement, societal, and conformity purpose. Therefore, providing a person with is a stronger comprehension of personal emotional eating.

Emotional Eating

There is a heavy emphasis in today's world on what we eat and the importance of exercise and for a good reason, because when you exercise and eat the right foods, it can be a major improvement in your life.

Our thoughts and emotional states can be the most excellent motivators of all. Thoughts and emotions are the forces behind much of our behavior, and if balanced, they can stabilize a healthy regimen in our diet and exercise patterns.

Being an Aware Eater

Being an aware eater means that you have more choices when it comes to choosing which foods you will eat, having a choice to eat or not, instead of overeating or eating in a compulsive or emotionally affected way.

What exactly is Emotional Eating?

Emotional eating is what happens when we consume or avoid food in order to mask or cope with our emotional experiences. The way people acted around food when we were young influenced our experience of it emotionally, and so emotional eating is a habit we learn from a very young age so it can be difficult to break, but with the help of self-hypnosis and self-awareness, it is possible to change these types of patterns.

Emotional eating is something everyone does every now and then, when it becomes an uncontrollable urge, that is when we must take action to change the habit of emotional eating. An important part of practicing self-awareness in emotional eating is not to mark it as right or wrong or good or bad. Practicing self-awareness in this area is merely calling attention to what is triggering the behavior, without judging the behavior.

Regulating Emotional Eating

To regulate emotional eating a therapist, healer or coach is very helpful in encouraging one to express one 's feelings in healthy and not destructive ways. This is one way to start developing awareness of your emotional eating patterns. Here you will start to view your feelings as feedback and as something to be heard and recognized, not something to be feared or to run away from.

A healthy awareness around emotional eating can also be created by using self-hypnosis and meditation to induce a trance state and use suggestions to reprogram the subconscious mind. Awareness is the key here; you can see that with it that you are more than your feelings, and without it, it can appear that you are overcome with your emotions and subsequent behaviors.

Issues With Emotional Eating

When emotional eating becomes an uncontrollable habit, it usually involves a whole host of deeply seated emotional issues.

In the sense of overeating, carrying additional weight on the body can serve an emotional purpose. An additional fat layer can give a sense of protection and be used as a tactic to create self-loathing or feelings of guilt. Many people may use extra weight to prevent intimacy with others and not to take responsibility for their lives.

  Regardless of the way we use emotional eating for weight, weight gain, or self-esteem, it is at a high cost to our mental wellbeing. We must discuss and become aware of the real issues which create our emotional eating habits.

A good way to start doing this is to become aware of your eating habits and behaviors. Do you eat even when you aren't hungry? Do you have a tendency to eat when you're frustrated, bored, depressed, or when you are experiencing negative emotions? Identify the emotions contributing to excessive eating.

Identify what else you can do to change this habit. Are there any actions you can take to recognize when you are triggered or are in the middle of an episode? Some solutions to break these patterns in a simple way can include talking to a friend, going for a walk, or finding something you want to do rather than eat. To ensure that this can be done, keep a list of alternative activities you can do when you are about to emotionally eat.

Dealing directly with the root of the problem is also very effective. By realizing the root of the issue, you can alter the subsequent effect of emotional eating.

Common Emotional Eating Causes

Emotional eating is a massive issue for many people who are struggling with their weight and typically demonstrates an unhealthy relationship with food. Once you understand what your triggers are, you will be able to break the pattern of emotional eating.

- Stress.
- Depression.
- Poor self-esteem.
- Unhappy with the body shape.
- Loneliness.
- Boredom.
- Financial worries.
- Relationship or marital problems.
- Greed.
- Lack of energy and inactivity.

Emotional needs are never met with a new green salad or large amounts of fruit. Emotional eating typically involves consuming excessively processed foods and sweet sweets like cake and chocolate. Let's look at ways to control the food relationship and avoid binge eating.

Efficient ways to avoid emotional intake

Keep an emotional journal and write down the periods when you feel like eating; you should begin to see a pattern that will help you to identify your triggers. You must find an activity that can replace eating at your most vulnerable moments. Exercise is a perfect way to lose calories, take shape, reduce tension, and feel good. Training does not have to be just lifting weights or hours in the gym, finding something enjoyable you are going to enjoy, such as a dance class or a badminton game. Also, learn to relax much more because stress often leads to poor nutrition. Take long walks or a relaxing bath and take some time for yourself every day. You will break with constructive action the process of emotional eating. Now that you know the common causes of emotional eating make lifestyle changes and stop those common triggers that make you overeat.

How to Treat Emotional Eating with Self-Hypnosis

If you can identify the reasons behind emotional eating, then you can easily manage your emotional issues and regulate your food intake.

Types of Emotional Triggers

- Emotional: Eating to reduce boredom, tension, stress, tiredness, depression, or solitude.
- Social: Social pressure from others, feeling awkward in social settings, or being around others who emotionally eat.
 - Environmental: Eating simply because there is a lot of food available where you are.
- Negative thinking: Eating because of negative thought patterns or habits. Self-hypnosis can be used to tap into the subconscious mind to reprogram these triggers. Also, a licensed hypnotist can help you to tap into your subconscious in order to reprogram negative beliefs, thoughts, and emotions that cause emotional eating. Hypnosis is a practical, non-pharmaceutical way to relax and relieve stress. You can program new ways of thinking and doing things to help you achieve your goals while training your brain to let go of past negative behaviors.

To begin self-hypnosis, write out the goals you would like to achieve. When starting out, stick to one goal on your list and write out affirmations or suggestions geared toward achieving this goal, which you will then communicate to the subconscious during the hypnosis session. Use phrases and terms that are meaningful to you in your affirmations.

One technique is to write them out as though your goal has already been achieved. For example "I am eating healthy", or "I am at my weight loss goal". Over the ages, hypnosis has enabled many people to accomplish goals that they might otherwise have missed out on achieving. You cannot only use hypnosis as needed for emotional eating but in this way can create your own personalized hypnosis practice for any other issues you would like to resolve with self-hypnosis.

Portion Control

When you eat rapidly, you do not notice your stomach's cues that it is full. Eat slowly and listen to hunger cues to enhance feelings of fullness and ultimately, consume less food.

Improved Digestion

Many folks are there: That moment when you are through with Thanksgiving dinner and suddenly regret eating the maximum amount as you probably did. Once a year may not be that big of a deal; however, often consumption of large portions will cause a disturbance on your gastrointestinal system.
Considerably larger portion sizes contribute to an upset stomach and discomfort (caused by a distended stomach pushing down on your other organs). Your gastrointestinal system functions best when it is not full of food. Managing portions can help to get rid of cramping and bloating after eating. You furthermore may run the danger of getting pyrosis; as a result of having a full abdomen will push hydrochloric acid back into your digestive tract.

Money Savings

Eating smaller parts may lead to monetary benefits, mainly when eating out. In addition to eating controlled serving sizes, you do not have to purchase as many groceries. Measuring serving proportions can make the box of cereal and packet of nuts last longer than eating straight out of the container?
Adult portion sizes at restaurants will equal two, three, or even more servings. Therefore, immediately the food arrives at your table, request a takeaway container and put away half of your food from the plate

How To Control Portions Using Hypnosis

Hypnosis can take you into a deeply relaxed state and quickly train your mind to understand when to do away with excess food instinctively, and allow your digestion to be lighter, and more comfortable. You may discover the pleasure of being in tune with what your own body requires nourishment. Hypnosis will re-educate your instincts to regulate hunger pangs. As you relax and repeatedly listen to powerful hypnotic suggestions that are going to be absorbed by your mind; you may quickly begin to note that:

- Your mind is no longer engrossed in food

- Your abdomen and gut feel lighter
- You now do not feel uncontrollable hunger pangs at "non-meal" times
- You naturally forget to have food between meals
- You begin to enjoy a healthier lifestyle

There is a somewhat simple self-hypnosis process for helping you control your appetite and portions. In a shell, you are immersing yourself into a psychological state and picture a dial, or a flip switch of some type that is symbolic of your craving and your real hunger. Then you repeatedly apply to develop a true sense of control, and then you employ it out of the hypnotic state and when confronted with those things and circumstances to curb the perceived hunger and control your appetite.

-Step 1: Find a comfortable position and one where you will remain undisturbed for the period of this exercise. Ascertain your feet are flat on the ground and hands not touching. Then once you are in position, calm yourself.
You can do that by using hypnosis tapes; they are basic processes to assist you in opening the door of your mind.

-Step 2: You may prefer to deepen your hypnotic state. The best and most straightforward is imagining yourself in your favorite place and relaxing your body bit by bit. Keep focused on the session at hand (that is, watch out not to drift off) then go to the third step.

-Step 3: Take a picture of a dial, a lever, or a flippy switch of some kind that is on a box or mounted on a wall of some sort- let it fully control your mind's eye. Notice the colors, the materials that it is created out of, and the way it indicates 0-10 to mark the variable degrees of your real hunger.

Notice wherever it is indicating currently- let it show you how hungry you are. Remember when last you ate, what you ate, whether or not the hunger is genuine or merely reacting to a recent bout of gluttony and wanting to gratify that sensation!
Once you have established the dial, where it is set, and trust that the reading is correct, then go to the subsequent step.

-Step 4: Flip the dial down a peg and notice the effects taking place within you. Study your feedback and ascertain that it feels like you are moving your appetite with the dial. The more you believe you are affecting your appetite with the dial, the more practical its application in those real-life situations.
Practice turning it down even lower and start recognizing how you use your mind to change your perceived appetite utilizing a method that is healthy and helps keep you alert when you encounter circumstances with plenty of

food supply. Tell yourself that the more you observe this, the better control you gain over your appetite.

You might even create a strong affirmation that accompanies this dial "I am in control of my eating" is one such straightforward statement. Word it as you wish and make sure it is one thing that resonates well with you. Once you have repeated affirmations to yourself severally proceed to the next step

-Step 5: Visualize yourself during a future scenario, where there is going to be constant temptation to continue eating although you are full, or to consume an excessive amount. See the sights of that place, take a mental note of the other people there, notice the smells, and hear the sounds. Become increasingly aware of how you are feeling in this place. Get the most definition and clarity possible then notice that once the temptation presents itself, you turn down the dial on your craving. You realize that you are not hungry to eat anymore, then repeat the positive affirmations to yourself a few more times to strengthen it.

Run through this future state of affairs severally on loop to make sure your mind is mentally rehearsed about your plan to respond.

-Step 6: Twitch your little finger and toes, then open your eyes and proceed to observe your skills in real life and spot how much control you have.

Practice the hypnosis for many days before going to face temptation, just to make sure that the process is firmly lodged into your mind. Unless hypnosis has positively compelled you or somebody close to you to shop for a new, smaller wardrobe, it is going to be arduous to believe that this "mind-over-body" approach may assist you in getting a handle on food consumption.

Seeing Is Believing Concepts

So, see for yourself. You ought not to be delighted by a number of tall tales of weight loss using hypnosis. The following concepts contain several suggestions for altering your diet, appetite, and serving portions.

Your Solution Lies Within

Hypnotherapists believe that everything you would likely need to succeed is within your reach. You do not want the newest drug or another absurd diet. Slimming is about trusting your innate talents, as you do while driving a car. You will forget how terrified you were for your first driving lesson. However, you maintained the lessons until you could drive without much thought or effort. Similarly, losing weight could appear beyond your reach; however, it is merely a matter of striking your balance.

What You Think You Can Achieve

This applies to hypnosis as well as real life. Subjects who expect results often receive them. The expectation of being helped is essential. You should think and expect your hypnosis weight loss strategy to work.

Intensify The Positive

Aversive or negative thoughts will work for a moment; however, if you hope for lasting transformation, you will want to assume a more positive demeanor. There is an exciting example of one 50-year-old woman who lost more than fifty pounds. She repeats daily: "Unnecessary food could be a burden on my body. I intend to shed what I do not need."

If You Visualize It, It Will Comes

Visualizing success prepares you for a victorious reality, much like athletes do. At the beginning of each day, images of clean, healthy eating help you imagine the required steps to turning into that healthy eater. Is imagination too burdening a task? If so, find a photograph of when you were at your most comfortable weight and start there. Try to remember your routines and find out what you can do differently at the present moment. Or perhaps visualize obtaining a recommendation from a future older, wiser self when she has necessarily attained her desired weight.

Send Away Food Cravings

Hypnotherapists habitually harness the ability of symbolic representation. Invite your mind to place food cravings on a white cloud or in a helium balloon and send them floating up, up, up, and away.

Invest In More Than One Strategy

When it comes to losing weight, a winning duo is cognitive-behavioral therapy (CBT) and hypnosis that helps work out harmful thoughts and behaviors. Raising awareness each smart hypnotherapist is aware of, could be a crucial step toward lasting change. Before attempting hypnotherapy, keep a record of everything you ingest for a week or two.

Modify As Often As Necessary

The importance of applying existing patterns has been emphasized repeatedly. Instead of submitting to a craving for a pint of ice cream, you can modify the calories craving to perhaps a cup of frozen Greek yogurt.

Unhealthy Relationships With Food

Too often we eat too much of what we need, and this can lead to unwanted weight gain.

Careful eating is important because it will help you appreciate food more. Instead of eating large portions to feel full, you will try each bite.

This will be easy for those who want to do it fast but need to do something to increase their willpower by extending the periods between their hours. It will also be very useful for people who struggle with food.

Controlling a portion alone may be enough for some people to see the natural results of their weight loss plan. Try your best to incorporate careful eating practices into your daily life so you can control how much you eat.

This meditation will be specific to eating an apple. You can practice careful eating without meditation, share your meals with others, or sit alone with a nice view out the window. This meditation will guide you to understand the types of thoughts that will be helpful while staying alert during meals.

Change your Mindset

The first step you must take on your weight loss journey is to change your mindset. This is the first and very important step to sustainable weight loss.

As you work to change your weight loss mindset, you are, in effect, rethinking what you really believe about losing weight, so that your overall weight loss journey serves you better.

In other words, you need to cultivate your own weight loss condition. This psychological change you must take can be even more difficult than adding a few additional herbs to your plate.

This is a thing that needs to be done. First of all, be aware that there are three words to keep in mind when embarking on this journey.

These words are "I can't", "I won't," and "I can't". These are three short words that you must ban to be successful, as they come from your mind and have virtually nothing to do with your inner strength or what you can achieve.

If you use them frequently, they can have a huge indirect effect on your weight loss journey and your level of fitness.

Therefore, you must reverse the entire scenario and leave the negative discussion behind. People trying to lose weight generally say so not just because of their past negative experiences.

For example, someone who says they don't like vegetables simply remembers old experiences that have nothing to do with their current behavior.

For this reason, their old experiences should not dictate their current behavior. If there are some that I can't or can't define in your vocabulary, you have to turn the script upside down and turn them into me and I can. This will motivate and encourage you to go further and after several days you will be able to choose your new rhythm with ease.

If your current fitness level is low, the words "I can't" will hinder your success. Instead of saying I can't do ten push-ups, let's just say I'm trying to succeed. You have to try, as it is better to try and fail than fail.

You can start with two push-ups and with each new day add one more push to go further until you reach your fitness goal.

Your weight loss journey should start by changing your mindset and rewriting your thinking to lose weight

There are many natural ways to overcome your weight loss plateau, such as changing your eating habits and being physically active.

However, without changing your mindset, these tricks will only work in the short term by providing a sustainable weight loss journey, as there is always an underlying thought that keeps you away from sustainable weight loss.

If you don't go there and face it, you will continue fighting along the way.

For example, many women tend to lose weight as soon as they begin to make healthier dietary choices, but their weight loss progresses to a halt before they are completely satisfied with what they see in the mirror.

The truth is that losing weight sustainably is much more than losing those extra kilos that seem to melt at the beginning of the journey.

The trick is to keep losing weight after this initial period. Many women fail at this step because, after periods of weight loss, their progress simply freezes.

The key reason for this to occur is that the very common weight-loss plateau prevents you from losing weight in the long run.

To overcome this problem, there is no magic trick you can do other than changing your weight loss mindset.

Overcome Your Weight Loss Plateau

The secret to overcoming your weight loss plateau is not in a secret diet plan or training program, but it is much deeper in your mind.

The first step you need to take to overcome your weight loss plateau is to identify the real reasons why you are overweight.

If you're overweight, the main reason is probably not a lack of exercise, but a lack of willpower or dietary choices.

Yes, these are all the factors that determine your weight and play an important role in your overall health, how your body looks and feels.

Though, these are the only certain manifestation of the deeper, real reason behind your weight struggles.

For instance, those fat resources in the bodywork as some kind of body protection. When we accumulate fat, we, in fact, build a massive fat shield in order to protect the body from various kinds of threats.

Moreover, many of us struggle with different fears, many of us feel threatened all the time both subconsciously and consciously. In these cases, the fat we accumulate may serve as a hiding point making us less visible and making us less noticeable, less shiny in the world.

Many individuals feel greatly disappointed in some areas of their lives, many of them feel as if they are not following any certain life purpose. Some of them are also greatly unsatisfied with their personal relationships and they feel no real connection with friends and family members.

These people struggling with threats and disappointments tend to hide behind their bodies and tend to fill their inner void by turning to food.

The truth is that there are many other psychological reasons for your weight struggles other than your dieting choices and your lack of physical activity.

As you work on changing your mindset, it is extremely important that you also work on identifying those reasons.

You must discover what is holding you back in order to get rid of those additional pounds for good.

Accept Current Reality

The next step requires that you truly accept your current reality. There are many females completely obsessing over their dieting plan, obsessing over counting calories, blaming their slow metabolism, and wondering what went wrong.

This is extremely unhealthy bringing nothing good. In fact, thinking obsessively about weight loss, hating what you see in the mirror, and thinking that your life would be much enjoyable if that excess fat were only a certain manifestation of the true thing that is keeping you from moving towards your goals.

Obsessing over these things, just shows that you are not accepting of your reality, that you resist it, and whatever you try to resist, it surely persists.

In order to overcome your weight loss plateau and to shred that stubborn excess weight, the first thing you are expected to do is to accept your current reality and work towards being okay with that.

This does not mean that you will stop your weight loss progress, but it means that by accepting your current reality, you can work towards a slimmer you in the future.

Once there, you will be completely free of those relative internal tensions which, once gone, make you more focused and motivated to keep reaching your goals.

Find Your Motivation

Many people, when thinking about the motivation for weight loss, what comes to mind is those media motivational weight loss posters with skinny models repeating washed out phrases we have heard many times before with no personal message.

These types of weight loss motivational posters are extremely superficial and, in many cases, even damaging.

Yes, they can motivate you for a short time period, but in the long run, this is not the kind of motivation you need to keep going.

Instead, you need to ask yourself what should be your own, your motivation without being conditioned by mass culture and media and their assumptions that being fit and skinny is what makes us happy and what makes our lives whole.

These assumptions in the majority of cases are not conscious at all and you should avoid them. Instead of resorting to mass culture and media, think about what is truly important to you, what your inner senses and connection are telling you.

Think about what you want to gain with your weight loss. Is it being full of energy or being completely confident in what you see in the mirror?

In pursuance of discovering your true weight loss motivation, you need to examine how you truly feel, you need to work on addressing your core values, and finally take complete ownership over your life vision.

Your motivation must come from you as your unique, personal manifesto, not from some fitness magazine or workout poster you see.

Once you have identified your own weight loss motivation, you need to embrace your core value and let your own, personal vision in addition to your desired feelings, guide you towards reaching your goals.

This kind of motivation comes from within you is the only right motivation you need and once you have it, everything else will come naturally.

The Virtual Gastric Band Program

The Virtual Gastric Band program is a Hypnosis strategy that reproduces the impacts, results, and advantages of a traditional gastric band or gastric bypass surgery. Initially created in Europe, the method requires no clinic remain or recovery period to acquire the ideal weight loss results. All change is designed, made, and actualized in the oblivious personality of the customer.

This healthy and regular choice of weight loss surgery has a 95% achievement rate. Analysts broadly perceive hypnosis as an extremely protected, consistent, and charming condition of profound physical and enthusiastic unwinding. The Virtual Band Hypnosis recommendations cause the oblivious personality to accept the stomach is a lot littler, the size of a golf ball, as though the gastric band was introduced precisely. It keeps the customer from over-eating and results in weight loss with a quantifiable decrease of muscle to fat and inches. However, there is no eating routine.

The motivation behind this hypnosis system is to assist individuals with eating littler bits and appreciate the solid changes they will naturally have the option to make, without hardship and consuming fewer calories. Most get-healthy plans include disposing of the nourishment's individuals cherish and can prompt disappointment because numerous individuals can't support an eating routine arrangement that makes them feel denied. At that point, they frequently eat more than they did before their "diet" disappointment and recover the weight. The focal point of the Virtual Gastric Band Hypnosis program isn't explicitly on what number of pounds are lost yet instead on dres's size decrease, the capacity to eat limited quantities of nourishment, and perceiving when one has had enough to eat, feel fulfilled, and quit eating. The typical result is that by eating limited nourishment quantities and halting when full, weight loss and littler apparel sizes will generally happen. Logically, it isn't easy to eat far less nourishment and not get thinner and apparel sizes.

Study Result

In mid-March and early April, two preliminaries started utilizing the Virtual Gastric Band program. One investigation bunch had five members, and the other had three members. The program comprised 4 hypnosis sessions, one every week for one month. Every individual was given the necessary "Golden Rules of Success" to track with specific Hypnotic proposals to diminish partition sizes, drink a lot of water just as inspiration to practice all the more frequently. All were told to tune in to an extraordinary pre-recorded hypnosis CD in any event once day by day for 28 days to help the positive, enthusiastic, and physical changes wanted. The goals of everything being equal and customers were to be and feel more beneficial, eat better and decrease their garments' size. A few members had diabetes and, additionally, pre-diabetic. All members were female and extended in age from the mid-30s to the late-50s. Most ladies had small kids at home, yet all were working ladies with occupied lives. Their weight loss goals ran from at least 40 lbs. To more than 100 lbs.

Session 2 Results

Multi-week after the first Virtual Gastric Band Hypnosis "surgery" session, each member revealed numerous positive changes, including a few changes not identified with proper dieting or weight loss. All members detailed they were progressively loose, ate little bits, drank more water, and saw their considerations, behavior, and feelings identified with nourishment and eating had changed significantly. The enthusiastic eating defined with every member or customer permanently halted by and large or was incredibly abridged. Most detailed, they perceived a "full inclination" and had the option to quit eating, usually. Some saw a deep-rooted propensity for eating immediately had changed. They ate all the more gradually and making the most of their nourishment more. One member acknowledged she never again wanted to eat ice-cream daily, which had been a propensity for a long time. Another took a large portion of her nourishment home from a café, which astonished her. Some detailed that they dozed better. One member, a pre-diabetic medical attendant with thyroid issues, never again wanted Chinese nourishment and turned out to be sick after eating a limited quantity of her preferred food, pasta. It was a reaction like what many experiences after a traditional surgical gastric band procedure. She conventionally would have had a few bits; however, one part was a lot for her. Her coffee utilization was decreased from 5 cups to under 1 cup every day. She lost 6 lbs.
Furthermore, she never again had overpowering desires for desserts or starches. Another member said she saw that "full signal" and now eats far less. Her garments fit her all the more serenely, and the fixation on nourishment is no more. Another saw that her preferred greasy, overwhelming nourishments didn't taste tantamount to what they used to. She is presently happy with far less nourishment, drinks load of water, and sees positive changes in her reactions and musings toward food.

Session 3 Results

Now, members had been tuning in to their CD for about fourteen days. All members announced it was simpler to eat little parts, eat all the more restoratively, dispose of enthusiastic eating, drink more water, and feel progressively loose. One lady quit her 1+ pack of everyday smoking propensity and didn't encounter withdrawal or passionate eating. Another quit her half-year nicotine gum propensity. There had been no proposals for halting smoking or consummation nicotine reliance during the hypnosis procedures. One individual lost 8 lbs. Another lost 4 lbs. in 10 days, without consuming fewer calories. Another lost 2 lbs. in any case, her garments fit her so much better that she believes she may have lost one full dress size. Everybody felt more in charge and ready to quit eating when fulfilled.

All except one individual experienced weight loss or having their dress fit all the more approximately, yet she announced that she was looser and more joyful than she has been in quite a while.

Session 4 Results

One preliminary group had encountered their final hypnosis session of the Virtual Gastric Band Hypnosis program. Most members in that group had encountered their hypnosis session also. Around then, different members had encountered only 3 sessions and a few just 2 sessions. That implies members had been utilizing the program and altering their behavior for only 3 a month and a half.

Everybody saw enhancements in their dietary patterns and decisions. Most eat all the more gradually, eat little bits, are increasingly loose, and have wiped out their enthusiastic eating. They feel definite and certain that the Virtual Gastric Band Hypnosis program has, at long last, permitted them to be in charge of their eating behavior.

The Virtual Gastric Band Hypnosis program helped every member and customer be in charge of their nourishment decisions and part size. Any individual who needs to eat more beneficial and shed pounds might be a contender for this new and specific Hypnosis program. When stoutness and the subsequent medical problems cost the American public and insurance companies millions, this might be a straightforward, unwinding, and fruitful approach to set aside money and lives without "going under the knife."

Virtual Gastric Band Hypnosis can be utilized by nearly any individual who wants to eat all the more restoratively to achieve weight loss goals in a characteristic and loosening way. It isn't essential to be a contender for the gastric band hypnosis program to use this entrancing methodology for change. The Virtual Band Hypnosis program is an amazing and regular approach to come back to a perfect load without surgery and deprivation.

Virtual Gastric Band Treatment

The virtual gastric band treatment is a new approach to the problem of morbid obesity. It combines elements of cognitive therapy and hypnosis with a technique called psychosomatic relaxation. The technique takes advantage of the natural tendency for obese people to feel hungry after eating and full after they have fasted. The goal is to use relaxation exercises and physical sensations as a distraction during meals, causing feelings of fullness sooner, which should lead to eating less at each mealtime.

The treatment is aimed at people who have tried and failed at diets or already had weight-loss surgery. It aims to help them reduce their food intake by 50%. The treatment is designed for people who have been deemed suitable for this kind of treatment. ?

What does virtual gastric band treatment entail?

The first step towards a virtual gastric band treatment usually involves a psychosomatic relaxation exercise. This step involves an awareness training program. It takes about three months to complete. You will be taught techniques like how to relax your body, how to relax your breathing and how to calm down your mind. You will also be told about techniques to cope with the emotional stresses in your life. You will also be taught how to go through a day without food, how to keep going when you are hungry and how to handle moments where you feel like giving up.

After that stage of the treatment, you will move on to the next step, which is the actual virtual gastric band treatment. This involves wearing a belt that has a device stuck between your stomach muscles (intragastric balloon). The device holds back part of your stomach so that it feels fuller for a longer period of time after eating. You will be connected to a machine that monitors how well the belt is working. This device is usually worn for 12 hours a day for six weeks in total.

The virtual gastric band treatment offers a new kind of approach in the fight against obesity. It combines three different approaches: hypnosis, cognitive therapy, and psychosomatic relaxation techniques. The combination of these three approaches has proven to be very effective in helping obese people lose weight.

At first, there was one researcher who thought about this new idea, Professor Bob Bloomfield, from Leeds Metropolitan University. As he explains in an interview:

The initial idea was to create a device that was invented by the gastric band and gastric bypass surgery, which is just a restriction device. So we wondered whether that would work. We asked people to wear them. The second thing, we got a lady hypnotist and we tried hypnotherapy. Then the third thing, the idea occurred to me that you could train people to use relaxation methods themselves.'

However, he admits that it took considerable time for his team of researchers to get this treatment going productively:

'This is not gold-plated stuff. You know, no one's making any money out of it whatsoever. I mean, it's a legal framework to bring it forward. You know, if we haven't made progress by the time, we've finished this degree of the research then we can't possibly get through a full university. That's the reason for this dip into hypnosis and hypnotism.'

In 1997 Bob Bloomfield and his co-researchers completed their research on the virtual gastric band treatment at Leeds Metropolitan University. They published their results in a medical journal called Diabetology and Metabolism. The article was accepted but then vanished from the journal altogether because of an error that was only discovered in 2013 - more than two decades after it was written.

In 2013, the article was reprinted in the British Medical Journal Open, with an apology from the editor for overlooking it all those years ago.

The paper presented the results of 15 patients who had undergone hypnosis or cognitive therapy using the virtual gastric band treatment. Of those 15 patients, 13 lost weight, and 12 of them were able to keep it off for a year after their treatment. The average weight loss was 10% in 6 weeks. One of the study's participants lost 30 lbs and kept off 100 lbs. for four years after taking part in this virtual gastric band treatment.

The study also explored the relationship between mind and body in a way that could benefit both obese people and people with diabetes. A lot of the participants in this study had diabetes as well. The patients who went into the hypnosis sessions lost more weight than those who went through cognitive therapy alone. Hypnosis helped them to curb their cravings, while cognitive therapy helped them to think about food differently.

Patients in this study had been suffering from morbid obesity for at least 2 years and they had failed to keep their weight off after diets. One man in the study said:

'I've tried every diet going but I've never got anywhere on them. I always just came back to my old ways of eating. I thought, if this causes any weight loss, then that's positive, but in the meantime, I've been gaining weight anyway.'

One of the patients in the study explained how she lost more than 50 lbs:

'I could really feel it taking effect. I felt like a different person. Every week when I went for a checkup, without fail it would be up a few more pounds... It started with ten pounds and by the end of the month, I'd lost 20lbs. The hypnotist told me that if I could keep doing it like that every week then pretty soon, I would have lost all my excess weight. That would have been fantastic, but I didn't manage it. But I did come back every week, and when they took the band off at my final check-up at five months, I had lost 30lbs. It was amazing.'

Some of the participants who took part in the study were not full-time workers, and some had opted to do a lot of their treatment outside of work. This showed that it is possible to access these treatments even if you are on a low income.

Self-Hypnosis Techniques

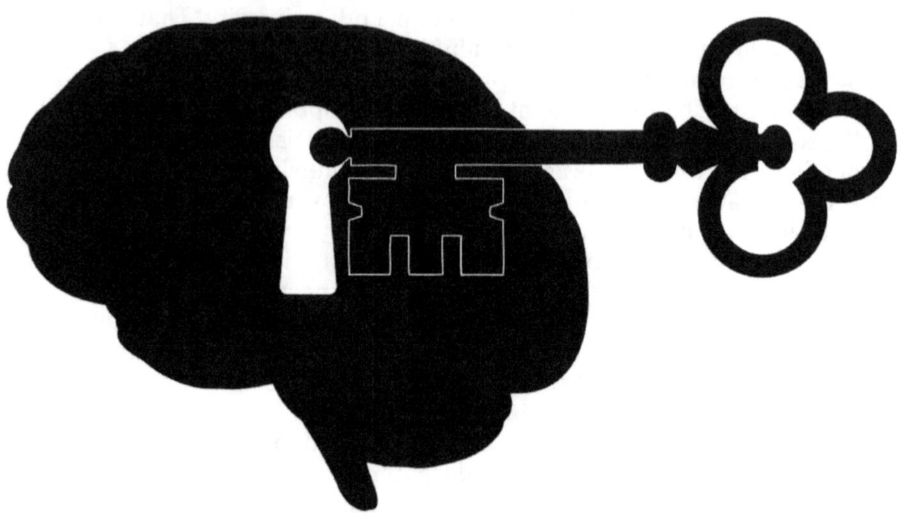

I will acquaint you with a straightforward, however powerful strategy of self-spellbinding. This procedure is called eye obsession self-entrancing and is one of the most mainstream and successful types of self-spellbinding at any point created. We will begin by utilizing it as a technique to enable you to unwind. After you have rehearsed these various occasions, we will include entrancing recommendations and symbolism. Decrease interruptions by going into a room where you are probably not going to be upset and killing your telephone, TV, PC, and so on. It is your time. You are going to concentrate on your objective of self-entrancing, and that's it.

At that point:

Sit In An Agreeable Seat With Your Legs And Feet Uncrossed

Abstain from eating a huge feast not long previously, so you don't feel enlarged or awkward. Unless you want to fall asleep, please sit in your seat because resting in bed may prompt you to rest. You may likewise want to extricate intimate apparel and remove your shoes. If you wear contact focal points, it is prudent to expel them.

 Keep your legs and feet uncrossed.

Gaze Toward The Roof And Take In A Full Breath
Without applying pressure to the neck or tilting the head back, choose a point on the roof and fix the appearance to that point. When you focus on this point, hold your breath for one second, and then breathe in again.

Quietly rehash the recommendation, "my eyes are damage and substantial, and I need to sleep now." rehash this procedure to yourself another couple of times and, if your eyes have not effectively done as such, let them close and unwind in a typical shut position. It is significant when saying the recommendation that you express it to yourself as though you mean it, for instance, is a delicate, mitigating, however persuasive way.

Allow Your Body To Unwind

Permit your body to turn out to be free and limp in the seat only like a cloth doll. At that point, gradually and with goal tally down quietly from five to zero. Disclose to yourself that with every single check, you're turning out to be increasingly loose. Remain in this relaxed state for various minutes while concentrating on your relaxation. Note the rise and fall of the abdomen and chest. Know how slack your body will become in any situation, try and relax it. In fact, the less you try, the more relaxed you believe.

At The Point When Prepared, Return To The Room By Checking Up From One To Five

Disclose to yourself that you are getting mindful of your environmental factors, and at the tally of five, you will open your eyes. Tally up from one to five out of an exuberant, enthusiastic way. At the enumeration of five, open your eyes and stretch your arms and legs.
Rehash this procedure three or multiple times and notice how each time you arrive at a more profound degree of unwinding. I hope to absorb the information contained in it, so I am determined to practice self-improvement all the time.
Some of the time, individuals will feel somewhat scattered or sluggish after they come out of the charming. It is like arising from an evening snooze, which is innocuous and goes after a couple of seconds. Be that as it may, don't drive or work hardware until you feel entirely wakeful.

Different Levels Of Brain Activity

Our brain is an entirely fantastic tool! It is made up of several billion cells that exchange information. These exchanges cause the emission of weak electrical currents - brain waves that can be captured by the electroencephalogram. The rhythm of these waves (measured in cycles per second) varies according to our activity: awakening, learning, rest, relaxation, light sleep, deep sleep.

The Beta Rhythm

It is the cycle of full awakening, the one we work on when we have our eyes open, and we are in action, we reflect, study, learn, etc. Our brain then works in full throttle, and the encephalogram shows us that it shows cycles in the range of 14 to 21 cycles per second. In hyper-activity states, our brains function much closer to 21 cycles/seconds than 14 processes.

The Alpha Rhythm

As soon as we have our eyes closed, we take a comfortable position, lying on a bed; for example, automatically, the encephalogram shows a slowing of brain waves, and our brain then operates at a rate that oscillates between 7 and 14 cycles/seconds.
It is interesting to note that at this rate, the two hemispheres of the brain manage to function together in perfect harmony whereas, during the Beta rhythm, we often operate with a dominant hemisphere (the left in most cases), which privileges analytical work and reflection but which "deprives" us of all the intuitive, creative and global perception of the right hemisphere.
But we'll go back a little further on the benefits of the Alpha rhythm.

The Rhythm Of Theta

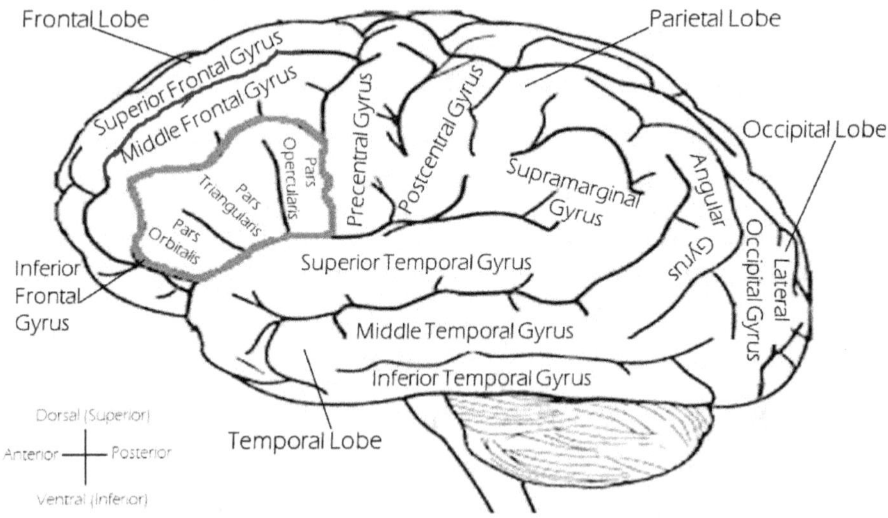

When brain activity slows down further, and we arrive in an area that oscillates between 4 and 7 cycles/seconds, we can say that the brain works at the rate of Theta waves. This rhythm corresponds to the phase of light sleep, and the deeper we sink into this rhythm, the deeper the rest becomes. At the Theta level, we also find the area corresponding to guided hypnosis and the size of pain insensitivity. It is, therefore, this level that we explore during deep hypnosis and regression sessions, and also that which is used in hospitals for anesthesia hypnosis.

The Delta Rhythm

It corresponds to the area of the unconscious, profound sleep, and the more we operate below four cycles/seconds, the more we fall into coma states that approach physical death. In this area, only vital functions are performed by the brain. When the encephalogram shows a flat path, it means brain death no longer had brain activity, and the individual is considered physically dead.

What Is So Special About The Alpha Level?

Let's go back to the alpha wave cycle, which we are particularly interested in since we can reach it alone through meditation, which is more difficult for the theta level, for which we need to be guided so as not to fall into sleep.
Why is this cycle essential to us? When we operate at alpha cerebral rhythm, our mind is calmer, and the two hemispheres of our brain function in perfect harmony (instead of usually having the rational left brain dominating), allowing us to have a more global view of things, which still allows us to:
·   To have a better concentration.
·   To have a better memory.
·   To be able to manage our stress and emotional states better.
·   to be able to take conscious control of the functioning of our bodies, organs, and physiological reactions.
·   to be able to take control of our habits, especially those we want to change.
·   To be able to create new, more positive, and healthy habits for our lives,
·   To find more creative and constructive solutions to conflicts or problems.
At the alpha level, we have a better perception of all our senses, and we are much more attuned to our intuition, which means that we know better what to do when we need to do it. Our mind is then "watchful" it interferes less often, and our choice is then fairer, more intuitive Intuition can be defined as this ability to know information that is outside our usual field of perception. She then communicates her messages to us through images, perceptions, voices.

The Four Alpha Level Sub-Levels

The alpha rhythm also breaks down into four levels:-
Level 4, very close to the state of awakening, activates automatically as soon as one takes a comfortable position, either comfortably installed in an armchair, or lying on a bed, and closes one's eyes. At that point, our brain automatically slows down brain waves. Then, if we persist longer, we feel our whole body relax. It's level 3 of the alpha rhythm.
At Level 3, our mind is still very active; we are still able to think of ten thousand things that concern us, then comes the moment when we feel like we're hovering. To be fair, we would be almost unable at that time to know what we were thinking is Level 2.
Then just after this phase, we sink a little more; we go through level 1, the necessary level of the alpha rhythm. Without even realizing it and because we are not aware of it, we fall even lower asleep. There are brain already works in Theta, and it's a shame because just before that, the opportunity was given to us at level 1, the necessary level of the alpha rhythm, to open the door of our subconscious and give him particular orders so that it serves us instead of helping us, as he often does
The purpose of exercises and methods of cognitive control at the alpha level, such as the Silva Method or personal active meditation exercises, aims to learn to reach level 1, to master it while regularly maintaining control and without falling further down in sleep. You could almost say that this is a sports exercise, although here the sport is purely cerebral. If I make this comparison with a joke, it is not entirely innocent because, as you know, the athletic performance will be directly proportional to the training you have done. So the more you train to work consciously at the alpha level, the easier it will be and the more valuable benefits you will get in all areas of your life:

- To improve your health
- To set professional goals and achieve them
- To work on your self-confidence
- To strengthen and develop your intuition
- To quit smoking
- Losing weight, etc.

Challenges Learning Self-Hypnosis

The harder you attempt to recollect the title, the harder it is to review. At that point, when you loosen up, the character returns to you. In some cases, when we make a decent attempt, we square ourselves from accomplishing our objectives. The mentality you take towards self-entrancing will decide how effectively you learn it. Acknowledge the pace at which you accomplish results, anyway little they may form the start appear. Have faith in yourself, and you will proceed to make the progress you want.

Post-Hypnotic Suggestions And Their Rules

As recently referenced, spellbinding is a condition of uplifted suggestibility. Giving yourself proposals when entrancing will empower an activity or other reaction to happen after the mesmerizing experience has happened. These types of recommendations are called post-mesmerizing suggestions and will assist you in achieving your objectives. Throughout the years, subliminal specialists have created rules of request. These are rules that will empower you to make the most significant progress with the proposals you give yourself. What follows is a synopsis of these principles.

Relaxation Techniques

Every human has their methods of relaxing, which can be unique and different from the general method others relax. However, relaxation is an essential part of our lives that we must not neglect. There are various relaxation methods, ranging from simple and easy techniques to complex techniques. So, you need to find the most suitable technique for you.

Tips to Relaxation

Relaxation is a very simple process, which is achieved by any means, yet you need a guide on how to achieve relaxation.

• Don't be too hard on yourself when you are trying to relax. Any relaxation method is to help you relax both your body and mind.
• Your environment must be quiet and free from distractions.
• Your position must be comfortable, whether sitting or lying
• Relax over few minutes firstly
• Have a routine of relaxation
• Be consistent
• Relaxation Technique
• Progressive muscle relaxation
• This simple means flexing, tightening, and relaxing your muscles by progression. You tense and then release these muscle groups one by one. For example, you tense and relax the muscles in the face first and which you move to the muscles in your hands, and arms. Another form of progressive muscle relaxation is passive muscle relaxation. You do not need to tighten or make the already tighten muscles tight any longer. You

just need to release and relax your muscles from the beginning of the technique.
• Imagery meditation or visualization help to relax your body and mind through the use of pictures
• Relaxation hypnosis
• Autogenic relaxation is the ability to imagine that some of your body parts, limbs especially.
• Other techniques include exercise, the use of the sensory organs to get relaxed. Deep breathing exercises and;
• Knowing which relaxation technique works for you is to try them at least.
• Relaxation Process
• Relaxation Hypnosis is a state whereby you enter into a great level of relaxation, by first quieting your conscious mind and allowing your subconsciousness to dominate more.
• Begin to have a good feeling all over your body as you sit in a comfortable position.
• You feel every nerve and muscle in your body is getting loose, and you are becoming relaxed
• You feel your arms getting relaxed and light
• This is a good feeling, and you are getting more relaxed gradually
• You feel a great sensation all over your body, from your head to your toes
• Let your muscle feel released and loose
• You begin to feel more relaxed, as you take each breath
• You begin to feel sleepy as you breathe in and out
• Deeper and calmer, you continue breathing in and out
• You are feeling very relaxed, and your muscles are loosed
• Your arm is getting lighter and relaxed. More relaxed as you hear your silent heartbeat.
• You are calmer as you breathe in and out, drowsier and sleepier.
• Progressive Muscle
• This exercise is to help you relax the muscles of your body. You will be asked to tighten your muscles and release them during this technique.
• Stay in a comfortable position, adjust until you feel really comfortable and the position is painless
• Close your eyes when you are ready, and breathe in through your nose. Take a deep breath, then hold your breath for a few seconds, and then exhale slowly.
• You begin to feel relaxed, at this point
• Hold your breath and then let go
• Allow yourself to become more relaxed
• Now, tilt your forehead, and raise your eyes up as though you are looking at the sky
• Raise your forehead, and you begin to feel tense, and tightened in your neck and head.
• You begin to feel relaxed

- Focus on your forehead, and now relax your forehead and notice the way you feel
- As you feel tension, you feel your mind wandering around, and you feel relaxed now
- Let all the tension drain and let go from you
- Let your eyes, nose, and face feel tensed, and focus on it.
- Begin to feel relaxed
- Breath in and out
- You feel relaxed, focus more relaxing
- Notice your mind becoming relaxed
- Now, focus on your jaw and smile widely. You feel your teeth clenched to each other, and now relax those muscles
- Relax your face and notice the feeling that comes from relaxation
- You feel comfortable, as your face and jaw become more and more released
- Relax your face a little more
- Breathe in deeply, hold your breath and breathe out
- Release your muscles and let go of your muscle
- Tense the muscles around your back, neck, and shoulders, but shrugging your shoulders and turning your neck
- Tilt your neck and feel the tension around your neck losing up
- Then move to your shoulders. Try to lift your shoulders to touch your ears, feel the tension in your shoulders and neck released, and now let go of these muscles
- Feel your shoulders becoming more comfortable
- Move your arms, and hold your hands together, raising your hands towards your shoulders. You begin to feel released and relaxed.
- Take a deep breath and then let go
- You feel the tension flow out of your shoulders, arms, and hands
- Relax your arms, hands, and shoulders.
- Now, focus on your breathing and abdominal muscles
- Take another deep breath through your nose
- Breathe in and out
- Feel the rising in your chest as you breathe out
- Repeat the action, breathe in through your nose, hold your breath and let go
- Notice the free relaxation you feel as you breathe out
- Feel the relaxation around our abdomen that has spread across your face, your hands, arms, and neck
- Relax as far as you can
- You feel as if you have a soft pillow behind your back, and you feel deeply relaxed
- Shift your focus on your shoulder, as though you want it to fall apart from your body towards your spine.
- Make your shoulders feel tense and let go now
- Let the relaxation spread into every muscle of your back
- Feel relaxed

- Take a breath in and out
- You begin to feel every pain in your back becoming released
- Go deeper into relaxing these muscles, and now tighten your abdomen
- Hold this position and now relax
- Soften your abdomen, feel your belly becoming more relaxed
- Relaxation is spreading across every part of your abdomen
- Tighten your lower limbs, the hips, thighs and down to your feet,
- Begin from your hips, feel the tension in your hips and release it now
- Take another deep breath and focus on your hips and thighs
- You begin to feel relaxed, and the tension in your hips is becoming released
- Then focus on your thigh, you feel it tensed, let go now
- You feel relieved, and the tension is released in your thigh
- Place your hands and your thigh and feel them becoming relaxed and softened
- Then move to your knee, at this point you tighten in your knees, let go of the tightened
- Focus on the relaxation
- You feel blood and oxygen rushing through your knees
- Release the knees and take another deep breath
- Let the relaxation spread deeper from your hips o your knees
- Now, we move to your toes and knees. Feel the tension in your toes and then feet
- Release your feet and toes, and you feel relaxed
- Move back to the ankle of your legs, try to turn your legs around
- Tighten the ankle for few seconds and let it go
- You feel the tension becoming released
- You feel more released, as you feel the relaxation spreading across your feet, toes, and ankles
- Feel the sense of reliving in your body as the tension is being released. Enjoy this relaxation
- Scan your entire body, allow your awareness to focus on each part of your body, and let every remaining tension be taken care of
- Scan your forehead, relax and feel released, move to your face, eyes, nose, and mouth, and let go of every tension
- Breathe in and out slowly
- Continue through every part of your body, your neck shoulders, chest, hands relaxed and released every tension
- Then your back, hips, abdomen, let go of every tension in the parts
- Then your knees, thigh, and toes, feel the tension in your body all wiped and flushed out of your body from your head to your toes
- Take a slow deep breath

Autogenic Relaxation

The autogenic relaxation technique involves generating relaxation within yourself and the body. The technique involves the individual relaxed, by imagining their body is warm and heavy.
This technique is to help your body feel warm and relaxed. And these are the steps
•	Find a comfortable position, you may choose to sit or lie.
•	Get settled into this position and try to notice the way your body. Simple notice the state of your body, and do not try to change anything.
•	Take a deep breath, in and out
•	Continue to take your breathing slowly
•	Begin to imagine your body becoming relaxed in the tensed areas
•	Focus your attention on your feet and get relaxed. Your feet are getting more relaxed now and warm, from the top of your feet to the sole of your feet
•	Shift your attention to your right foot, feel the top and sole of your foot.
•	By now, you begin to feel a sensation of warmth and heaviness together in your feet, and the sensation begins to increase deeply.
•	This sensation moves down to your ankles and legs and spreads across your toes; by now, you are more relaxed than at the beginning of the technique.
•	Shift your attention from your legs to your hands
•	Focus on your right hand; feel the warmth spreading across your fingers and thumb, which is spreading across both of your palms.
•	Focus on your left hand, too, feel the warmth spreading across the fingers, to the thumb, and the palm.
•	By now, your both hands are completely warm, heavy, and relaxed
•	The warmth spreads across your wrist, and lower arms.
•	You feel the sensation around your elbow, upper arms, wrists, and shoulders.
•	You begin to feel deeply relaxed, and these parts feel heavy and very warm.
•	Shift your attention to your feet and legs, you begin to feel warmth in your feet and legs, and this warmth is spreading across your lower legs, to the knees, joints, upper legs, thighs, and then to your joint.

Increase Self-Confidence

Establish where you are now

You should take a full-length picture of yourself at present as a push mechanism from your current position. Two primary factors are relevant to health. One is whether you like the image you see in the mirror and the second is how you feel. Do you have the energy to do what you wish, and are you feeling strong enough?
Explore your reasons for wanting to lose weight. These are what will keep you going even when you don't feel like it.
Assess your eating habits and establish your reasons for overeating or indulging in the wrong foods.
It is assumed that you have the desire to get healthier and lose weight. Here, you state clearly and positively to yourself what you want, and then decide that you will accomplish it with persistence. Use the self-hypnosis routine explained above to drive this point into your subconscious mind.
Determine your motivation for the desired results, and how you will know when you've accomplished the goal. How will you feel, what will you see, and what are you likely to hear when you achieve your goal?
Devote the first session of self-hypnosis to making the ultimate decision about your weight. Note that you must never have any doubt in your mind about your challenge to lose weight.
Plan your meals every day. Weigh yourself frequently to monitor your progress as well. However, do not be paranoid about weighing yourself as this can actually negatively affect your progress.
Repeat to yourself every day that you are getting to your ideal weight, that you've developed new, sensible eating habits, and that you are no longer prone to temptation.
Think positively and provide positive affirmations in your self-induced hypnotic state.

Tweak Your Lifestyle

Every little thing counts. If you want to lose weight and lose weight, this is an important thing to pay attention to. Making a few changes in your regular daily activities can help you burn more calories.

Walk more

Use the stairs instead of the escalator or elevator if you're just going up or down a floor or two.

Park the car one mile from the destination and walk. You can also walk briskly to burn more calories.

During your rest day, make it more active by taking your dog for a long walk in the park.
If you need to travel a few blocks, save gas and avoid traffic by walking. For greater distances, dust off that old bike and pedal your way to your destination.

Watch how and what you eat

A big breakfast kicks your body into hyper-metabolism mode so you should not skip the first meal of the day.

Brushing after a meal signals your brain that you've finished eating, making you crave less until your next scheduled meal.

If you need to get food from a restaurant, make your order to-go so you won't get tempted by their other offerings.

Plan your meals for the week, so you can count how many calories you are consuming in a day.

Make quick, healthy meals so you save time. There are thousands of recipes out there. Do some research.

Eat at a table, not in your car. Drive-thru food is almost always greasy and full of unhealthy carbohydrates.

Put more leaves, like arugula and alfalfa sprouts on your meals to give you more fiber and make you eat less.

Order the smallest meal size if you really need to eat fast food.

Start your meal with a vegetable salad. Dip the salad in the seasoning instead of pouring it on top.

For a midnight snack, munch on protein bars or just drink a glass of skim milk.

Eat before you go to the grocery to keep yourself from being tempted by food items that you don't really plan to buy.

Clean out your pantry by taking out food items that won't help you with your fitness goals.

The whole idea in the tweaks mentioned is that you should eat less and move more. You may be able to think of additional tweaks. List them down together with the ones found in this book.

Will Gastric Band Hypnotherapy Work For Me?

There are numerous diverse kinds of hypnosis that aid the human body in different ways. Some of these methods include hypnosis for weight loss and healthy living, which are different types of hypnosis for weight loss. Gastric band hypnotherapy is one of them, and popularly known as a type of hypnotic state that is suggested to your subconscious, which involves fitting a gastric band around your stomach. This in return, helps you lose weight, along with general hypnosis for weight loss sessions.

This type of hypnotherapy is often considered the final type of hypnotherapy people try if they would like to reach their goals. The practice involves surgery known as gastric band surgery. During surgery, a gastric band gets fitted around the upper part of your stomach, with the purpose to limit the total amount of food you consume daily. This is a more extreme type of hypnotherapy for weight loss, which has proven to help people lose weight. Since it is surgical, you cannot carry out this method yourself. It also includes potential risks, which is why it must be treated with respect and only carried out by a certified medical practitioner.

You can, however, implement gastric band hypnotherapy yourself. It is a technique most commonly used by hypnotherapists with the purpose to trick the subconscious into believing that a gastric band has been fitted when in reality it hasn't. Since hypnotherapy is focused on putting your conscious mind on silent, and implementing thoughts and beliefs in your subconscious mind, as a type of hypnotherapy, it is quite effective. Given that hypnotherapy offers us many benefits, as well as allows us to imagine and come to terms with what we are capable of doing, it acts as the perfect solution to reaching some of your goals that may seem out of reach.

Gastric band hypnotherapy involves the process of believing that you have experienced the physical surgery itself, ultimately making you believe that the size of your stomach itself has been reduced too.

The gastric band used in gastric band fitting surgery is an adjustable silicone structure, used as a device to lose weight. This gastric band is used during surgery and placed strategically around the top part of your stomach, leaving a small space above the device. The space left open above the gastric band restricts the total amount of food that is stored inside the stomach. This is done to implement proper portion control every day and prevents overeating. The fitted gastric band physically makes it difficult for one to consume large amounts of food, which can set you in the habit of implementing proper portion control daily. This will essentially cause you to feel fuller after eating less, which in return encourages weight loss.

Most people choose to have the surgery after they've tried other methods to lose weight, including yo-yo dieting, diet supplements, or over-the-counter drugs, all with the hope to lose weight. Gastric band surgery acts as a final resort for those who desperately want to lose weight and have been struggling for a long time.

Gastric band hypnotherapy serves as a very useful method as it can allow you to obtain a similar result as the gastric band fitting surgery itself. That's because you are literally visualizing getting the same procedure done and how you benefit from it. During gastric band hypnosis, you are visualizing yourself losing weight subconsciously, which translates into your conscious reality.

Hypnotherapists that specialize in gastric band hypnotherapy focus on finding the root of what prevents their clients from losing weight. Most of the time, they discover that emotional eating is one of the leading causes that contribute to people holding on to their weight. They also make a point of addressing experiences that remains in your subconscious mind but is yet to be addressed. These experiences often cause people to turn toward unmindful and emotional eating, which then develops into a pattern that feels impossible to kick.

Since stress is added to our lives every day, and people don't stop and take the time to process feelings or perhaps not even give them a thought, most turn to food for comfort. This also plays into emotional eating, which has extremely negative effects on the body long-term as it also contributes as one of the leading causes of obesity.

Given that obesity is an incredibly bad illness, and more people get diagnosed with the condition every day, it is something that needs to be addressed. If gastric band hypnotherapy can prevent it or restructure our thinking patterns to not act on our emotions, but rather invite and process it, then it is a solution that everyone who needs to lose weight should try. Once a hypnotherapist learns about why you're struggling to implement proper portion control, they will address it with the virtual gastric band treatment at a subconscious level. During this visualization session, you will have imagined that you have undergone the operation and had the gastric band placed around your upper stomach. This will lead you to think that you feel fuller quicker, serving as a safer option as opposed to the surgery.

How Gastric Band Hypnotherapy Works

Hypnotherapy for weight loss, particularly for portion control, is great because it allows you to focus on creating a healthier version of yourself safely.

When gastric band-fitted surgery gets recommended to people, usually because diets, weight loss supplements, and workout routines don't seem to work for them, they may become skeptical about getting the surgery done.

Nobody wants to undergo unnecessary surgery, and you shouldn't have to either. Just because you struggle to stick to a diet, workout routine or lack motivation does not mean that an extreme procedure like surgery is the only option. In fact, thinking that it is the only option you have left, is crazy.

Some hypnotherapists suggest that diets don't work at all. Well, if you're motivated and find it easy to stick to a diet plan and workout routine, then you should be fine. However, if you're suffering from obesity or overweight and don't have the necessary drive and motivation needed, then you're likely to fail. When people find the courage and determination to recognize that they need to lose weight or actually push themselves to do it but continuously fail, that's when they tend to give up.

Gastric band hypnotherapy uses relaxation techniques, which are designed to alter your way of thinking about the weight you need to lose, provides you a foundation to stand on and reach your goals, and also constantly reminds you of why you're indeed doing what you're doing. It is necessary to develop your way of thinking past where you're at in this current moment and evolve far beyond your expectations.

Diets are also more focused on temporary lifestyle changes rather than permanent and sustainable ones, which is why it isn't considered realistic at all. Unless you change your mind, you will always remain in a rut that involves first losing, and then possibly gaining weight back repeatedly. Some may even throw in the towel completely.

Since your mind is incredibly powerful, it will allow you to accept any ideas or suggestions made during your hypnosis gastric band hypnosis session. This can result in changing your behavior permanently as the ideas practiced during the session will translate into the reality of your conscious mind. By educating yourself on healthy habits, proper nutrition, and exercise, you also stand a better chance of reaching your weight loss goals sustainably.

The gastric band fitting procedure will require a consultation with your hypnotherapist where you will discuss what it is you would like to gain from hypnotherapy. After establishing your current health status, positive and negative habits, lifestyle, daily struggles, and goals, they will recommend the duration of hypnotherapy you will require to see results. During this time, you need to inform your hypnotherapist of your diet and physical activity history. They are likely to ask you questions about your current lifestyle and whether you changed it over the years. If you've lived a healthy lifestyle before, then they will try to find and address the reasons why you let go of yourself and your health. If you have always lived your current unhealthy and unbalanced lifestyle, they will trace it back through the years with the hope to discover the reasons behind it. During your initial session, your weight loss attempts, eating habits, and any health issues you may experience will be addressed. Your attitude toward food will also be acknowledged, as well as your relationship with it, with people, and your surroundings.

Now your therapist will have a better idea of the type of treatment you need. The procedure is designed to have you experience the gastric band surgery subconsciously, as though it has really taken place. You will be talked to in a deep, relaxed state, exactly the same as standard hypnosis. During this session, you will be aware of everything happening around you. Suggestions to help boost your self-esteem and confidence are often also incorporated into the session, which can also assist you in what you would like to achieve consciously.

You will be taken through the procedure step-by-step. Your hypnotherapist may also make theater noises to convince your subconscious even more. After your session, your hypnotherapist may give you self-hypnosis guides and techniques to help you practice a similar session for the results to become more effective. Sometimes, gastric band hypnotherapy only requires a few sessions, depending on what your needs are.

Gastric band hypnosis doesn't only involve having to go to physical hypnotherapy sessions, but it also requires you to implement some type of weight management program that specifically addresses your nutrition, addiction, and exercise habits. It addresses habits between your body and mind and helps you implement new constructive ones.

After gastric band hypnosis, you can expect to feel as though you have a much healthier relationship with food, as well as a more mindful approach in everything you do. During the visualization process of gastric band fitting surgery, you will come to believe that your stomach has shrunk, which will trick your brain into thinking that you need less food. This will also make you think that you don't need a lot of food, which will make you more acquainted with consuming healthier portion sizes.

Gastric band hypnotherapy is successful as it makes you think that you are full after eating the daily recommended amount of food for your body. It is also considered much healthier than overeating or binge eating. You will learn to recognize the sensation of hunger versus being full, which will help you articulate between the two and cultivate healthier eating habits.

Detailed Exercises To Effectively Install Gastric Band With Hypnosis

Preservatives Industrially prepared foods, sweeteners, even flavor enhancers are entirely different from the foods our ancestors ate. Our body has no idea how to digest them, and in many cases, they cause hormonal chaos, which activates your process of accumulating fat. We do not ask you to give up all junk food. If you incorporate more organic and healthier food into your diet, you can balance you're eating habits.
Stress daily
Whole books are written about this topic. We don't need to explain much to know that anxiety What causes us daily stress is the leading cause that you eat after hours, satisfying that anxiety by using your body as a garbage can.

Mental Hunger

Your body only understands one form of hunger, and it is physical hunger. Emotional blockages cause us to hunger mentally. You can starve yourself in an emotional or mental sense. You may starve for love, fun, joy, intimacy, life experiences, or a deeper spiritual connection. These mental and emotional cravings can trigger the same chemical signals in your brain as the physical causes of hunger. Feast profound city the fear of not having enough money, or of losing something you value, can send the message to your body that resources are limited, but the only resource the body understands is food. As far as your body is concerned, the only thing you can accumulate is fat. Any fear that resources may be limited is interpreted as fear of famine, and your body will accumulate as much fat as it can, "just in case."

Emotional obesity

You may not even be aware of it. Still, if on some mental level, you have associated the idea that being fat makes you more confident, or that it somehow serves an emotional need, giving you a tremendous hidden positive benefit (such as not hurting you), you suffer from "emotional obesity." It is one of the cases in which your body is right, and your body is protecting you. It makes you feel more emotionally secure. After your hands touch, you will lower your arms, take a few deep breaths, and open your eyes again. When you open them, you will already be much more relaxed than before, your imagination heated up, then look at a fixed point right into your eyes, and start several times to breathe deeply and retain the air in your lungs, we will do it five times, with your eyes open as long as you can keep them open. Then you will relax each part of your body until you are entirely relaxed, physically, and mentally. Here the journey begins. You will imagine yourself at the top of an ancient staircase, descending as you listen to me count from 10 to 1. Once down, in more profound levels of your mind, you will go through a door in front of you, to enter your ideal resting place, a beautiful place full of nature.

After enjoying heating the visualization, you will imagine waking up the day you operate, waking up in your bed, to go to the hospital, where you will be received by the receptionist who will give you the pertinent indications to perform the gastric band operation with hypnosis. You will enter the corridors of the hospital, visualizing people, listening to their whispers, until you get to your room. You will change your clothes, and the surgeon will come and ask you to mentally sign a consent document, the same that you will sign in this book. Once done, he will take you to the operating room, where he will perform the intervention. You will even listen to the sounds of the monitors measuring your vital signs. As you will see, it is practically the same as in reality, but using all the power of your imagination, to change the associations. Negative influences of your unconscious and allow yourself to slide into weight loss. Perform this exercise two or three times during the first week.

Emotional Unlocking

The induction is very similar to the previous one until reaching the ideal resting place. All the exercises are similar, but this one, in particular, is designed so that you understand that there are two parts of you, one that has made you accumulate fat in your body, driving -dows obesity. Still, this part contains a positive benefit for you, which you don'. It knows yet, and another part of you, which led you here, to find an alternative to your project to improve your quality of life. In the exercise, I will ask your unconscious to send you some signal, through images, symbols, emotions, words, or any representation, to identify the positive benefit you obtain with the malicious behavior that made you fat. Once identified, you will try to think of new alternatives that give you an equal or better benefit, to avoid that malicious behavior of eating more than necessary, even if you do not find alternatives, with the sole fact of recognizing that a part of you, caused that fattening, to give you some positive benefit, to help you, considerably advanced in your development. Then we will continue with positive suggestions to help accelerate the natural process of weight loss. Do this exercise two or three times during the second week.

Release of Obstacles Throughout our lives, we encounter obstacles every day. Human life is endless with obstacles. Still, you could free yourself from them to see only the objectives you want to achieve. For this, Iván developed this exercise. Imagine a giant hot air balloon, shaped like a stomach, anchored at the end of a path in your ideal resting place. Next to the hot air balloon, you will have a bench with several colorful stones, giant scissors, and a marker. You will take a seat, and you will write in a few words, all the obstacles that you think prevent you from reaching your goal, on the stones. Then you will place the stones in the globe, and with the scissors, you will cut each of the ropes that keep the globe attached to the earth, as well as the obstacles attached to you, to see them move away completely towards the infinite horizon, disappearing forever from your life. Then we will continue with the positive suggestions for your benefit. Perform this exercise two or three times during the third week.

Life Choice

In the last exercise of the first month, we will make a conscious choice about two paths that we can choose, one with our previous life, with the path full of garbage, fast food, candy papers, and the other path full of healthy trees and fronds, vigorous animals, many natural colors and clean and pure oxygen. So that you see yourself crossing the path you have chosen, representing the new stage of your life. Then we will continue with the positive suggestions. This exercise is done all or three times during the fourth week.

Adjustment of the gastric band

This exercise, with the same induction of the implementation of the band, is to adjust the gastric band in the hospital where it was implemented, in case you continue to eat more, to fill yourself up faster, you should do it only two or three times during a single week, approximately one month and a half or two months after starting the Gastric Band with Hypnosis program
The motivation for exercise is excellent audio that cheerful use two or three times a week to motivate yourself with some fun visualization exercises, so that you naturally want to exercise, without thinking about the effort, being able to start enjoying life in another way, much healthier and more natural.
Reinforcement of suggestions
This audio should be used every day for a month, to help your body accept the suggestions effectively. If you can do it some time, continue to the next, but do it more than you can.

Night Exercise

An exercise designed to enter a natural sleep, accepting positive suggestions, and leading to a night of profound sleep, you will notice that day after day, you wake up with more optimism, more desire to doing things happier. This exercise alone has made more than 100,000 people lose weight, becoming one of the most visited on YouTube. It is based on the Gabriel Method, whose book I highly recommend. Do this exercise every night for a month.

Self-Hypnosis For The Sense Of Safety

(put music with binaural sounds)

Choose a quiet, noise-free environment.

Sit or lie down comfortably.

Close your eyes.

(pause 3 seconds)

Make contact with the breath.

Allow my voice to guide you through this process.

(pause 5 seconds)

Inhale through your nostrils, mentally counting to three.

One.

Two.

Three.

Hold your breath.

Exhale from the nostrils, mentally counting to four.

One.

Two.

Three.

Four.

(pause 5 seconds)

Inhale and mentally repeat: "While inhaling, I relax" and meanwhile observe the flow of breath.
(pause 5 seconds)

Exhale and mentally repeat: "While I exhale, I relax" and meanwhile observe the flow of breath.

(pause 5 seconds)

Inhale and mentally repeat: "As I inhale, I relax more and more" and in the meantime listen to the sound of breathing.

(pause 5 seconds)

Exhale and mentally repeat: "As I exhale, I relax more and more" and meanwhile listen to the sound of breathing.

(pause 5 seconds)

As you inhale, repeat mentally: "As I breathe in, I relax even more" and meanwhile I contract the muscles of my arms and legs.

(pause 5 seconds)

As you exhale, mentally repeat: "While I exhale, I relax even more" and meanwhile relax the muscles of the arms and legs.

(pause 5 seconds)

There is a door in front of you.

You open it.

Exit the door and you're on a beach.

(pause 10 seconds)

The sky is blue, cloudless. Feel the sound of the light wind. See the seagulls sliding in the air.

(pause 5 seconds)

The sand is white, warm underfoot.

(pause 5 seconds)

Look at the sea. It is calm, serene, peaceful.

(pause 5 seconds)

As you watch it, you also feel calm, peaceful, calm.

(pause 5 seconds)

You start walking on the beach, towards the water. You feel the warm sand under your toes and you feel satisfied, you feel satisfied.

(pause 5 seconds)

Inhale deeply through your nose. Feel the scent of salt and sea. It fills you with freshness.

(pause 5 seconds)

It satisfies your body, mind, and soul.

(pause 5 seconds)

You came to the water. Feel the wet sand and then the water that caresses your feet and ankles. It is warm and soft like sand.

(pause 5 seconds)

Even the waves have a soft, sweet, satisfying sound.

(pause 5 seconds)

Each wave that melts on the sand satisfies you even more. It satisfies you even more.

(pause 5 seconds)

When the wave withdraws, your dissatisfaction withdraws.

(pause 5 seconds)

You start taking a walk along the beach and enjoy every step you take.

(pause 5 seconds)

You keep walking and you enjoy every sensation.

(pause 5 seconds)

There is nobody on the beach except you and you feel perfectly at ease.

(pause 5 seconds)

In front of you see a large, comfortable mattress.

(pause 3 seconds)

You can't wait to lie down.

(pause 2 seconds)

You can't wait to savor the pleasure of total fulfillment.

(pause 3 seconds)

You lie down on the large and comfortable mattress and immediately savor the feelings of joy and well-being.

(pause 5 seconds)

You continue to enjoy the sound of the wind and waves.

Continue to enjoy the softness of the mattress.

Continue to enjoy the delight of this moment.

(pause 5 seconds)

You always feel happier.

More and more satisfied.

More and more satisfied.

(pause 5 seconds)

You hear the sound of the waves, and every wave that arrives on the beach satisfies you more and more. It satisfies your body.

It satisfies your mind.

You are satisfied with the spirit.

(pause 10 seconds)

Bring attention to the head.

(pause 5 seconds)

Feel how the whole head is completely satisfied.

Sated.

Satisfied.

Of this being here and now.

You don't need anything.

(pause 5 seconds)

Open your mouth slightly and let the jaw relax.
Your mouth is full.

Your language is full.

Your throat is full.

You don't need anything.

(pause 5 seconds)

Bring attention to your arms.

Feel how they are loose, stretched, from shoulders to fingers.

Do you feel OK?

You do not need anything.

(pause 5 seconds)

Bring attention to your legs.

Relax them even more.

(pause 5 seconds)

Bring attention to your back.

Feel how loose, relaxed, from the neck to the buttocks.

You always feel better.

You realize that you need nothing more than this well-being.

(pause 5 seconds)

Bring attention to your chest.

Let her relax even more.

(pause 5 seconds)

Bring attention to the stomach.

It is sated. Joyful. Happy.

(pause 5 seconds)

Bring attention to the abdomen.

It feeds on this feeling.

Of this well-being.

Of this pleasure.

(pause 10 seconds)

Enjoy the well-being of being free from every need.

(pause 5 seconds)

Enjoy the pleasure of being satisfied.

In the body.

In the mind.

In the soul.

(pause 5 seconds)

Your every cell feeds on well-being.

Your every cell is satisfied.

Satisfied.

Satisfied.

(pause 5 seconds)

You are satisfied.

Satisfied.

Satisfied.

(pause 5 seconds)

Understand now your wonderful well-being.

(pause 5 seconds)

You are like this beach, these waves, this mattress.

(pause 5 seconds)

You are a satisfied and satisfied person in any situation.

(pause 5 seconds)

Feel how easy it is to let go of all your worries and needs.
(pause 5 seconds)

Feel how easy it is to be satiated and satisfied.

(pause 5 seconds)

Continue to feel the sense of satiety.

(pause 5 seconds)

The sense of satiety expands in your body, in your mind, in your soul.

(pause 5 seconds)

The sense of satiety pervades every hour.

Every minute.

Every second of your day.

(pause 5 seconds)

Prepare now to enter an even deeper fulfillment state.

Get ready to make this feeling of perfect satiety your main feeling.

(pause 5 seconds)

Continue to lie on the soft mattress of this sweet beach.

(pause 5 seconds)

Now the sun is about to set on the horizon.

(pause 5 seconds)

Observe the line of the sea that meets the sun in the distance: as the sun sets, I will count from ten to one. When I get to one, the sun will be completely set and you will be completely and perfectly satisfied. Completely and perfectly satisfied.

Ten

The sun begins to set on the horizon. Note how the colors change, while the sun begins to drop: note the orange of the sky, the blue and green of the water, how they mix together. Your feeling of well-being mixes with these colors.

Nine

The sun goes down on the horizon and you feel full of well-being.

You feel yourself floating in this well-being.

Eight

The sunsets behind the horizon and you feel the sense of satiety descending in the mouth, in the tongue, in the throat.

Seven

The sense of satiety descends into the chest, stomach, abdomen.

Six

The colors still change. The water is now a calm golden mirror and you feel this way too.

Calm and bright. You are confidently abandoning yourself to the current.

Five

The sense of satiety descends into the pelvis, genitals, legs.

Every part of your body lets itself go more and more to this sense of satiety.

Four

As the sun goes down more and more, you feel this perfect sense of satiety throughout your body from the tip of your head to the tip of your feet.

Three

You are completely at peace.

Two

Float in this sense of satiety.

One

You keep floating in this sense of satiety.

(pause 5 seconds)

With this satiety, it is easy for you to lose excess weight. Because now you know you don't need to eat more.

(pause 5 seconds)

Now you know it's not the food that satisfies you.

Now you know that what satisfies you is this well-being.

(pause 5 seconds)

Now you know it's not the food that relaxes you.

What relaxes you is this well-being.

(pause 5 seconds)

Now you know it's not the food that gives you security.

What gives you security is this well-being.

(pause 5 seconds)

Now you know that it is not the food that satisfies your needs.

What satisfies your needs is this well-being.

(pause 5 seconds)

Now you know it because you know it.

You know why you feel it.

Why do you live it?

(pause 5 seconds)

You will bring this satiety and this sense of well-being into your life and with this satiety, from now on, it will be easy for you to maintain the right weight.

(pause 5 seconds)

Continue to float in this sense of well-being and satiety.

Feel how this sense of well-being and satiety is part of you.

Feel how this sense of well-being and satiety is you.

(pause 5 seconds)

Now bring this feeling of perfect satiety into your everyday life.

Join the index and thumb of the right hand and the left hand.

Anchor the feeling of perfect satiety to this finger gesture and bring it into your life.

(pause 10 seconds)

Keep holding your index fingers and thumbs together and allow this feeling of perfect satiety to flow through you.
(pause 10 seconds)

Whenever you join your index fingers and thumbs together in your waking state, you will instantly reactivate this feeling of perfect satiety and you will feel it flowing in you instantly.

(pause 5 seconds)

Whenever you feel the feeling of hunger outside ordinary meals, you will join your index fingers and thumbs and instantly reactivate this feeling of perfect satiety.

So you will feel perfectly satisfied, instantly.

(pause 10 seconds)

From now on, in the waking state, you will spontaneously associate the sense of hunger with this gesture, which will instantly satisfy you.

Separate your index fingers and thumbs.

(pause 5 seconds)

You are about to return to the waking state.

Prepare to bring every word you have heard and every feeling you have to wakefulness.

(pause 5 seconds)

Your subconscious mind will process every word you have heard and bring it into your everyday life.

(pause 5 seconds)

You will want to listen to this audio and every time you hear these words, the suggestion will become more and more powerful for you.

(pause 5 seconds)

Whenever you hear these words again, the suggestion will become an increasingly important part of you.

(pause 5 seconds)

Every time you hear these words again, you will become more and more the person you have chosen to be.

(pause 5 seconds)

Mentally repeat:

"I will count from one to five and at the end of the count I will feel completely awake and better than before."

(pause 5 seconds)

One.

(pause 3 seconds)

Two.

Mentally repeat:

"I am about to return to the waking state, which means that even in the waking state my subconscious will continue to carry out the instructions I have given it."

(pause 5 seconds)

Three.

Repeat mentally: "Soon I will open my eyes."

(pause 3 seconds)

Four.

Repeat mentally: "Every day I will feel more satisfied and satisfied".

(pause 5 seconds)

Five.

Open your eyes.
You are now fully awake, feeling good, feeling better than before.

(Turn off the music with binaural sounds)

Final tips

Remember to repeat this self-hypnosis constantly following the program.
The subconscious works out of habit and habit are formed with repetition.
Repetition is therefore essential for the program to work in the best way.

I also suggest that you immediately test the functioning of the anchor. Put
your index fingers and thumbs together and feel the sensation of satiety
flowing inside you.
It must be activated clearly, you must have full sensation.

Self-Hypnosis To Achieve Goals

To alter actions, feelings, and perceptions, self-hypnosis is also used. For example, to better deal with the challenges of daily life, people often use self-hypnosis. Self-hypnosis can improve confidence and also help individuals learn new skills. It can also be used to help combat habits such as smoking and overeating, as effective stress and anxiety relief. With self-hypnosis, sportsmen and women may boost their athletic performance, and people with chronic discomfort or stress-related disorders also find it beneficial (hypnosis should only be used in this way after a medical diagnosis has been made and under the guidance of a doctor or qualified therapist).

This approach is called self-hypnosis of eye fixation and is one of the most common and efficient types of self-hypnosis ever developed. We are going to begin by using it as a way to help you relax.

We will incorporate hypnotic prompts and visualization after you've done this a number of times. By moving into a room where you are unlikely to be interrupted and shutting off your phone, TV, screen, etc., eliminate disturbances. It's your turn here. You will concentrate on your self-hypnosis target and nothing else.

Then:

1. With your legs and feet uncrossed relax in a relaxed chair.
Right before you consume a big meal, stop consuming it because you don't
feel bloated or awkward.
Sit in a chair because you intend to drift off as laying down on a bed is
likely to cause sleep. You may want to loosen your tight clothes as well and
take your shoes off. It is advisable to remove them while you are wearing
contact lenses. Hold your feet and your legs uncrossed.

2. Look up at the sky, then breathe deeply.
Pick a spot on the ceiling and focus your eyes on that point without
straining your neck or tilting your head to the far back. Take a deep breath
and hold it for a moment and then breathe out as you keep your eyes
focused on that spot. "Repeat the "My eyes are sleepy and heavy and I want
to SLEEP NOW" recommendation quietly. Repeat this procedure to
yourself another couple of times and if your eyes have not already done so
let them shut and relax in a regular closed position. When
you say the idea, it is important that you say it to yourself as if you mean it,
in a soft, calming yet persuasive way, for example.

3. Let your body relax.
Just like a rag doll, cause the body to become loose and limp in the chair.
Then count down quietly from five to zero, slowly and with intent. Tell
yourself that you are getting more and more comfortable with each and
every number. When concentrating on your breathing, remain in this calm
state for a period of minutes. Note how the diaphragm and chest are rising
and dropping. Be mindful of how calm the body is without ever trying to try
to calm it. Probably, the least you try, the more you feel comfortable.

4. Come back to the room when ready, by counting from one to five.
Tell yourself you are more conscious of your environment and you can
open your eyes at the number of five. In a colorful, enthusiastic way, count
from one to five. At the count of five, open your eyes and extend your arms
and legs.
Three or four times, practice this technique and notice how you achieve a
deeper degree of relaxation each time. If you notice, though, that you do
not sleep as much as you would like, do not push it. In order to perform
self-hypnosis on a daily basis, there is a learning curve involved.
When they come out of the hypnosis, people can often feel a bit spaced out
or drowsy. It is close to waking up from an afternoon sleep, and after a few
minutes, it is innocuous and passes. However, before you feel fully awake,
do not drive or control machinery.

How to Set Your Self-Hypnosis Goals?

1. Give a high priority to meeting your targets. Project on a regular basis to use self-hypnosis and you will continue to see progress.

2. On paper, set down your priorities. Clarify and be clear on what you plan to focus on. Be sure that you have targets that are attainable. It could be useful to break them down into manageable measures if they are long-term targets.

3. Formulate and write down the hypnotic ideas. Write up a range of recommendations for the objective you are focusing on. Ignore the guidelines for ideas that are post-hypnotic. You might even want to write a script of your own.

4. Decide the imagery you are going to use. If your intention is to relax, imagine on a warm summer's day a fun scene like a beach or a park. You may want to use imagery of consequences as Mandy did.

5. Do not give yourself a hard time if you fail to fulfill a task. Note, failure to fulfill a task does not mean that you are a failure. You may need to tackle the objective in a particular manner, or maybe you need to be persistent.
Difficulties Learning Self-Hypnosis
Have you ever noticed the annoyance on the tip of your tongue of needing a name? The more you try to remember your word, the harder it would be to remember it. Then the name returns to you as you rest. Often, we block ourselves from completing our targets because we push too hard. The mindset you have towards self-hypnosis will dictate how quickly you master it. Don't try too hard or set goals that are impractical. Relax and find time for yourself. Respect the speed at which you produce outcomes, however, limited they might appear at first. Believe in yourself and you will continue to achieve the desired results.

Self-Hypnosis in Medicine

There are amazing examples that illustrate how effective self-hypnosis can be. Take the recorded example of Victor Rausch (1980), who was experienced with hypnotic treatments by a dental surgeon. Rausch used self-hypnosis as his only anesthesia when he needed surgery to remove his gallbladder.
More recently, science has demonstrated that self-hypnosis instruction can help patients solve a number of health issues. They include:

Anxiety: After studying self-hypnosis strategies, patients who underwent heart surgery reported reduced levels of anxiety. A review of children with cancer found less fear and behavioral disturbance associated with surgery after practicing self-hypnosis.

• Pain: after practicing self-hypnosis methods, patients with multiple sclerosis (MS) showed lower levels of chronic pain than those who did not. In comparison, a study in children found that functional abdominal pain was relieved within three weeks after a single self-hypnosis session.

Tension Headaches: Self-hypnosis therapy has lowered the incidence of tension headaches in children and teenagers. Long-term headache pain relief by self-hypnosis was seen by another study in adults.
Chronic dyspnea: In adults with trouble breathing at rest, single self-hypnosis instruction relieved symptoms within one month in 13 out of 16 patients.
Irritable Bowel Syndrome: IBS patients have been shown to be able to boost the effects of IBS as well as the Low FODMAP exclusion diet gold standard.

An effective technique for changing the mind is self-hypnosis. It is an incredibly secure approach that can offer increased self-esteem, trust, assertiveness, and relaxation. During stressful periods, self-hypnosis can also be used to help relieve the effects of psychiatric problems, such as irritable bowel syndrome, nausea, pain, and headaches.

Self-hypnosis is a way of placing oneself in a state of trance so that you can give yourself constructive feedback. Putting yourself into a trance might sound challenging, but it's really not as complicated as it seems. As human beings, throughout the day, all of us go in and out of mild trances. You also go into a mild trance state when you fall asleep at night.

The human brain relies on brain waves, and beta waves are considered the usual "waking" brain waves. Alpha waves are the next step down, followed by theta waves and then delta waves. The quickest waves out of all four are beta waves, with the slowest being the delta waves. (If you are curious, the Greek alphabet letters do not order brain waves from quickest to slowest, but in the order in which the brain waves were discovered.) You want to come from beta to alpha and preferably down to theta to carry yourself down to a trance state. You don't want to go into the delta all the way back, or you're going to fall asleep.

The many benefits of self-hypnosis

Self-hypnosis presents the body and mind with many advantages. The most noticeable positives are the improvements that you will be able to achieve in your life because of the constructive feedback that your subconscious mind incorporates.
Improved sleep, better healthy hormones, and decreased stress are other advantages.

Advantages of Self-hypnosis:

• Can be achieved everywhere.
• Subjects can feel more managed.
• Hypnotic recommendations are chosen by the subject.
• Saved money from the consultancy fee.
Advantages of Hypnosis with a Hypnotherapist:
• It could be easier to reach the Hypnotic State.
• The psychiatrist is free to choose constructive ideas.
• The session could be more formal.
The psychiatrist is qualified to see things (your "blind spots") about you that you don't.

10 Weight Loss Myths

I will unlock the top weight loss myths in the shortest answers with the greatest potential below:

Have you ever felt like you were doing everything that you were being told to do to lose the extra pounds?
Well, you are not alone. The media controls so much of your thinking sometimes it is hard just to make the right decision. There is a lot of information in the world on weight loss, but every one of us struggles with making the right choices. The myths are the highest misconceptions I have found in my career of 15 years as a professional trainer. Use them immediately in your daily routine. To have success you not only have to have the right information, but you will also need determination and motivation. You hold the power in you to get started now.

Myth 1- If, I work out with weights I will get big and bulky
The only way to get big and bulky is to continue to have bad eating habits. You need to find your resting metabolism. How much food do you need to consume to be healthy, lose weight, and feel great? You have to try really hard on any person to get your muscles to grow. It is the last thing to worry about. Focus on using a set of muscles a day to work out to burn the maximum number of calories. A recovered muscle will always outperform a tired muscle. That means fewer calories burned for you if your muscle is tired.

Myth 2- Just doing cardio will give me the best fat-burning result. Although cardio stands for heart lungs. It does not mean the most powerful fat burner. In fact, the harder you push your body in one sitting or workout with the same exercise the more likely of using your muscle tissue for energy versus fat stores. Look at fat burning in the 3-day window. Not today. Even if that program worked. The biggest downside would be that your lungs expand to a new level EVERY 10 minutes. That means from the very first day you start losing your ability to burn as much fat...If, you can't figure out why you have skinny legs. It could be from too much running. That may crash your metabolism. How long can you actually be a marathon runner? Some may try, but at the same time, it is not very likely you. It takes a lot of time to train for a marathon. We are talking 50 miles a week! Not to mention the wear and tear on your connective tissue. I am not against long runs. It feels good. It's just not my whole game plan.

Myth 3- You need to work your whole body every day
Your body needs time to adjust. Your body does all of its replacing and dropping while you are asleep. Around 90% of any result happens when you are sleeping. Not when you are awake.

Your body will adapt to any workout you do every day. Fast adaptation will warrantless results. You want to pick a large and small muscle group per day. Attack it with a lot of energy. Wash and repeat that process weekly. When you come back weekly you will be stronger. Giving you a better fat-burning workout each time. Too much overtraining happens when you do the same muscles or exercises every day.

Myth 4- Liposuction will give me the answer I need
The truth is you will more than likely be right back to where you started. What? How is that? Well, your plastic surgeon can only take off so much at one time. Most of the time that magic number is a WHOPPING ten pounds. After your surgery, you can't move for 3 weeks. I do not care what they tell you. I have seen it over and over. Since you can't do anything your body slows down. So, anything you eat stays with you. I have seen people actually gain weight. Have not met one person that said they wanted it again. Not to mention that you have to rub or massage your bruises so water does not get trapped between your skin.

Myth 5- Fat is bad for me
The fact is fat has two meanings. One is the kind you eat. That has a few different names within that. Then their body fat. Cells or adipose tissue. They are not the same. Your body fat is stored food. With maybe some water. End of question. The body does not care whether or not is it's a carbohydrate, protein, fat, or anything else the body did not burn off. Dietary fat has taken a bad rap. In my eyes and 15 years of experience-fat is really not even our problem with our foods. In fact, you will need fat in your body if you do not want to age quickly, or you want to drop body fat, keep hormone levels balanced out, repair muscles. Otherwise, your body is missing some pieces of the puzzle. It is not balanced. It does without any doubt carry more calories per gram than the other major macronutrients. They are carbs and proteins.

Myth 6- All carbohydrates are bad for me
You will need them to balance your blood sugars. Which is the key to dropping body fat and energy? Not mention not feeling depressed. If you do a no-carb or ketogenic diet you will find out really quick what it's like to feel like dirt without carbs. You don't have to do this!
Always know how your food is harvested. Then what happens on each stop of its way to your table. If it was originally brown and now it is white, something is missing. To the body, it is not the same food anymore. The name of the food does not matter. Your body breaks food down. It can be called wheat bread, even have colored added to the bread, and if it is processed and bleached. It is not the same. Real wheat will not cause weight gain. It will not cause weight gain.
Processed weight will almost always cause weight gain.
Are you starting to see the picture?

Myth 7- Rice, wheat, and grains are bad
It does not matter the kind of food it is. It matters what happens to the
blood sugar once you eat the food. The average consumer buys food that is
broken down already or is using sugar for a preservative. The two hot diets
out Paleo and raw vegan neither eat any kind of processed food. Let the
light flash for a minute. Ok. Brown rice is your friend. As long as it is not
instant.

Myth 8- Red meat is bad for me
It is what the meat has been processed in is what is bad for you. Maybe it
has been pumped full of hormones. When you add white processed bread
to a heavily processed fat. That's your combination for a heart attack.
The absolute highest food in vitamin A is red meat liver.
A burger from a fast food place can get you in trouble. It has been heavily
processed in all ways. Preserved and over-processed.

Myth 9- Your metabolism is slow
That is another word that has multiple meanings. Your metabolism is your
ability to break your food down. Storing your food is another process. The
slower the food breaks down the less of a chance there is to store that food
or some would call it energy.
Most likely your body breaks down food fine. Honestly, I have never seen a
real case where your body does not break the food down correctly. There
are other situations that may cause issues. When someone messes with
your hormones that can have a dramatic effect on weight. Just at all costs
stay away from messing around with hormones. Your body will become
different at that point. More importantly, you may always be stuck taking
that hormone or thyroid medication.

Myth 10- I only need to focus on my calorie intake.
Yes, the amount of food you consume does affect your ability to lose fat.
The kinds of food are just as important if not more important. What your
body does with the food once it is inside you is the real question. Can your
body burn this food up or does your body need to repair? If, not it will
store. I have seen firsthand when a person gets a lap band and gets great
results. Eating less than 1000 calories a day. Then after a couple of months,
the body adapts to that 1000 calories. Now, what are you going to do?
A lap band is a band around your stomach that is surgically put there. It
shuts off your signals to want to eat. It makes your stomach smaller. Make
sure you put the kind of food before how much of food. Surround yourself
with the proper kinds of food.

What Food Should I Avoid?

When you are going on any kind of diet, it is important to make sure that you are avoiding the right foods. If you are on the diet plan and you continue to eat a lot of the foods that you are supposed to be avoided, then this kind of defeats the purpose and is going to make it almost impossible for you to lose weight and see the results that you are looking for out of the way. That is why we are going to spend some time looking at the foods that we should avoid when it comes to the fat-burning diet and the foods we should avoid when it comes to the low-carb diet. Being able to put these two together and learning what foods are good for us and which ones we need to avoid can make all of the difference in the health benefits that we are able to get.

Foods to Avoid on the Fat Burning Diet

The first part that we are going to take a look at here is some of the foods that you are able to work with when it comes to the fat-burning diet. To start, even though carbs are allowed on this diet plan, you do need to be careful about the kinds of carbs that you are eating. You want to focus on this diet with lots of whole grains, whether that is bread or pasta, and you get lots of healthy fruits and vegetables as well.

However, you do need to avoid a few types of foods during this time, especially if you are on one of the lower-carb diets. In some of these, you need to avoid things like white and processed carbs. That means the white pieces of bread and kinds of pasta, and the baked goods and sweets are all things that we need to avoid when we go through this kind of diet plan as well. Stick with the healthier options, and you will do a whole lot better when you are on this diet plan.

Another thing to cut out is processed and fast foods. Sure these taste amazing and can make life a little bit easier when it comes down to the busy nights with your family. But when you are working on losing weight and improving your health, and when you are on the fat-burning diet, these are things that you need to avoid. Make sure that you are cutting these out as much as possible, and if you can, consider just not having them at all. The beverages that you are allowed to have on this kind of diet plan will vary as well. Things like water, tea, and milk are the best choices for you to have. You can have a few fruit juices on occasion, but make sure that they do not come with a bunch of bad things or extra sugars in them, and consider watering them down to make them a bit better as well. You want to make sure that you are as hydrated as possible and avoid things like sodas and pops and all of the sports drinks and other things that are going to ruin your health.

Remember, both the fat-burning diet and the low-carb diet are all about helping you to eat foods that are healthier and wholesome for the whole body. Doing this is going to ensure that you are set up for success and that you will be able to lose the weight that you want, while also improving the other aspects of your health. If you are not careful about some of the foods that you are consuming and you eat the ones that are bad for your body, then you will not be able to get the good health that you need.

ヨルクの味わい際立つ
EXTRA CACAO
MILK CHOCOLATE
Choco
Creamy milk and the richness of cacao
New Standard Chocolate
Choco

Foods to Avoid on a Low Carb Diet

Now that we have had a chance to talk about some of the foods that you need to avoid on your fat-burning diet, it is time to move on to the low-carb diet. You will find that there are a lot of similarities in foods that you should avoid between these two diets, which is going to make them even easier to follow when you go through and use them well. But often the low carb diet is going to be more restrictive than some of the other options, so we need to keep that in mind as well.
The first type of food that we need to avoid is grains and slices of bread. Throughout the world, bread is going to be a common food that a lot of cultures like to eat. There are a lot of types of loaves of bread that we are able to enjoy, but many times the amount of carbs in these is going to be high. Both the bread that is manufactured with refined sugars and the whole-grain bread will be higher in carbs, and when you are on this kind of diet, you will need to cut down on these because they are likely to hold onto way more cars than you are supposed to eat during the day.

You will also need to be careful with the amount of fruit that you eat. While this is not completely off the table, you may find that there are a few types of fruits that will not be recommended because they are going to come with a higher content of carbs in them. Sweet and dried fruits are going to be the biggest culprits here. For example, having about .25 cups of dates will be somewhere between 20 and 33 grams of carbs, but a small banana would have closer to 18 grams.

Most vegetables are going to be fine in moderation, but again, we need to worry about some of the starchy vegetables that we are eating. The majority of the vegetables that we will want to eat are going to come with a higher fiber content so that is good for helping us to control some of our levels of blood sugars and for weight loss. But this is not going to extend out to all of the vegetables that we are looking at. Some of the vegetables that are considered starches are going to contain more cars than fibers and that is why we need to limit them as much as possible on this kind of diet plan. There are a lot of great vegetables that you are able to enjoy when it comes to being on a low-carb diet, and you can enjoy them as long as you monitor your carb intake. Some of the vegetables that you need to watch out for because of the carb content will include things like beets, yams, sweet potatoes, potatoes, and corn. Some of the better options that you are able to work with and will provide you with fewer carbs and more nutrients will include mushrooms, lettuce, cauliflower, avocados, spinach, and green beans.

There are also a few other grains that we need to watch out for when we are working with the low-carb diet. We want to be careful with pasta even though it comes in a lot of diverse types, and it is not expensive to work with. It is going to come with a high amount of carbs in it though and this is not a good thing on this kind of diet plan. You will find that a cup of pasta that has been cooked will be near 40 grams of carbs and whole wheat is only slightly better with 31 grams of carbs. The best alternative that you are able to use in your meals for this one is spiral zed vegetables or shirataki noodles.

Cereal should be avoided as well. Most of these are going to be full of sugar, and that is not going to do you any favors when you are working with the low-carb diet. You will also find that oatmeal, which is an option that is usually seen as better and healthier than some of the others, is going to still come in with 28 grams of carbs that we need to worry about.

Next on the list is going to be the juice. This is one of the biggest mistakes that you can make on this kind of diet plan. Yes, the juice is going to come in with a few nutrients that we are able to work with, but there are a ton of carbs and sugars that we need to deal with, and this is going to cause a huge increase in our levels of blood sugars along the way.

For example, there are upwards of 48 grams of carbs that are found in every 12 ounces of unsweetened apple juice. A bottle of regular soda is only going to come in with 39 grams in comparison. And it gets worse. If you are working with that same size but in grape juice, there could be up to 60 grams of carbs, which is already above what most low-carb diets are going to allow you for the whole day.

These are going to provide us with a ton of nutritional benefits that are so good for us. These legumes and beans are going to come with high fiber content, and they are great at helping with heart complications and inflammation as well. However, we have to remember that they are going to have a higher amount of carbs.

This does not mean that we need to get rid of the legumes and the beans completely. It is often going to depend on what we are doing for the rest of the day. Depending on how many carbs you have in a day, or plan to have, you may be able to eat a small amount of these legumes and beans. But you need to plan it all out and be careful in the process.

And finally, we are going to need to be careful about the milk that we consume. If you would like to get some of the good nutrients that your body needs, like the B vitamins, calcium, and potassium, then we need to make sure that we drink milk. But when we are on a low-carb diet, it is often best to go with a plant-based option or something else. This is because an eight-ounce serving of milk is going to come in with 12 to 13 grams of carbs that we need to worry about, and that is never a good thing.

As we can see with both of these diet plans, there are a lot of things that we will need to limit ourselves on and that we are not allowed to have in the first place any longer. This can make it really hard to follow this kind of diet plan and can cut down on what we are able to consume. Make sure that before you get started on this kind of eating plan for some of your own needs.

How to Create the Ideal Sleep

Environment

Trying to sleep in a setting that is not conducive for you can be quite a task. Unless the environment around is set up just right, you may keep tossing and turning in bed until you reach a point of exasperation. Sometimes we set ourselves up for failure by ignoring a couple of conditions that might significantly influence our sleeping patterns. If getting some sleep is among your topmost priorities, making sure that you set up a pleasant environment can leap you to depths of sleep you could never imagine. Here are some things you need to do without switching up your room:

Make the Bed Comfortable

If you have been sleeping on the same mattress with a significant depression at the center for the last 20 years, there is a big chance you can barely score any sleep. If you wake up with a stiff back and the feeling of the tire, yet you seem to enjoy sleeping in other places, you might need to replace that mattress. This goes for the pillows too. If you keep shifting them during the night, it might be time to get a new one.
The thought of the expenditure might be a considerable blow to deal with. Still, if it comes between you and getting a good rest, I suggest preferring the latter. We all spend a massive part of our day lying in bed to achieve some sort of relaxation. It is only fair to give ourselves a good experience, as sleep itself is essential for our daily functioning. If purchasing a new

mattress and pillow seems like a huge amount to cough up now, there are other natural methods applicable online that can be of help.

Keep the Right Temperature

Do you regularly stay up at night because you cannot stop sweating? Do you receive sleep interruptions when you wake up in the middle of the night to change your sweaty clothes? It would be a good idea to observe what level of temperature serves you best before you sleep next time. Research has it that when your body is preparing itself for slumber, the temperatures drop significantly. Keeping your room cool can provide a conducive environment for you to achieve the level of rest you require. A good tip would be to sleep with no clothes on. It increases the chance of a good night's sleep, but it also works by reducing any temperature build-up that the body might experience.

Keep It Quiet

Unwanted sounds are also some of the most critical thieves sleep has ever seen. The source of the disturbance may not matter. The idea that there is a source of distress in the first place is the only thing that has to alert you. The noise of whatever magnitude can severely affect your sleep cycle. Watching out for this disturbance and trying to eliminate it can be of great help to achieve sound sleep.
Getting a sound machine can be a good leap to counter this. Audio devices get fame from their smooth lulling sounds that drown all the other surrounding sounds. It can help in creating a soothing environment for someone to sleep. If the thought of sounds, in general, does not sit well with you, getting earplugs can do the trick.

Do Away with Gadgets

Placing your digital alarm clock a bit far from your view is also something to look into. Most people who have insomnia keep getting a lot of disturbance from the light. To make the torment more for themselves, they keep checking the time and only panic when they see how much time is fleeting. The best idea would be to face it away from you at a distance from the bed. This way, you will not get late to wake up because you will always have to stand to put off your alarm.

Clear the Clutter

You do not need to keep your room stocked up like a gym. Aiming for a clean room with nothing else but your bed and clothes can improve your sleep. Having so many things in your bedroom other than what you need to sleep on will only make your mind associate the room with them. Now your bedroom will not be a place to sleep; it will be a place to study, play games, and hike on the mountain of clothes on the floor.

Keep It Dark

Artificial light mimics natural light while emitting a blue light that keeps people awake. An excellent way to achieve sleep would be to keep the room as dark as possible. Having heavy blinds to counter any outside light is highly advised. It also means you need to get rid of light emitters such as glow lamps and night-lights.
If eliminating your cellphone from your room does not seem so reasonable, always keep it screen-side down and on silent. When phones light up with new texts and emails, your sleep is bound to be distracted, and your attention is captured as well.
You might end up using the time to get sleep to check on your emails-which is not what we want.

Aromatherapy

Research has shown that it can help to encourage sleep by using certain scents in a room. What aromatherapy does is create a pleasant and calming atmosphere that can assist you to settle down. It's also nice as part of a routine that your brain will pick up as a cue that it's almost time to go to sleep through ongoing use. Lavender and vanilla are some of the recommended scents to use.

Make Your Sleep Environment Quiet and Comfortable

One thing you should always do if you are having trouble sleeping is to make sure that your sleep environment is safe, quiet, comfortable, and otherwise conducive to your personal needs for peace and relaxation.

If your children are the problem, get them to modify their behavior. If neighbors are the problem, see what you can do to enlist their cooperation and support. If the telephone rings late at night, try to muffle the sound, turn off the ringer, or instruct friends and relatives not to call after certain hours.
If minor noises tend to bother you, consider using constant background noise to help you get to sleep.

Some people find that an air conditioner, fan, vaporizer, dehumidifier, or other mechanical device helps to block out other distracting influences, such as noisy neighbors.

Darkness

If you are required to sleep during the day, too much light in your sleeping environment can be a problem. If this is true for you, consider buying thicker curtains, installing window blinds, or wearing a blindfold.

Clocks

If you are having trouble sleeping, it is best not to focus your attention on the time. This is one of the bad sleeping habits that can become a "secondary" cause of insomnia. Looking at a clock every 5–10 minutes while you are lying in bed or glancing at the clock to see what time it is each time you awaken during the night are unnecessary behaviors that should be avoided. To help you do this, consider making the following changes in your sleeping environment:

- Keep clocks and other time cues away from your bed!

- No light-emitting clocks

- No ticking or chiming clocks

- Remove wristwatch at night

- Remove wall clocks or any other time device in the bedroom

If you need a clock for an alarm, get an electric one and put it out of sight (hide it under your bed, in a drawer, or cover the clock face or turn the face away from you).

Avoid focusing on the time or putting yourself under time-pressure of any kind.

Temperature

Make sure the temperature in your bedroom is conducive to your needs. If not, consider installing an auxiliary heater, ceiling fan, air conditioner, fan, electric blanket, etc. If your temperature requirements differ from those of your sleeping partner, consider negotiating to arrive at a mutually satisfying arrangement.

General Comfort

Is your mattress comfortable? Is your pillow too soft or too hard? Would you sleep better in separate beds placed side-by-side? Would you sleep better in a queen-size or king-size bed? These and other questions of comfort should always be addressed.

Hypnotherapy and Insomnia/Sleep Problems

In minimizing or treating insomnia, hypnotherapy may be very effective, although not all forms of insomnia are vulnerable to hypnotic care. Hypnotherapy may not respond well to insomnia induced by biological disorder, sickness, or medication effects. However, if the key causes of your insomnia are stress and anxiety, then hypnosis, together with proper sleep hygiene, can well provide an efficient cure.

Sleep Hypnosis

What is Insomnia?

Sleep is something that everybody needs. In both our physical and mental wellbeing, it plays a crucial part. But sleeping disorders, such as insomnia, can make having enough sleep difficult for certain people. Lack of sleep, as well as making you feel exhausted, will lead to physical illness, and increase the risk of heart disease. Mentally, not having enough sleep will lead to anxiety and make focus difficult for you.

Insomnia is described as trouble trying to sleep or remaining asleep long enough for the next morning to feel refreshed.
When you can't manage to fall asleep, most of us will have experienced a night of disturbed sleep and will know how it feels. You may be worried for the next day or you may have had a cup too close to bedtime. You might find it easy to fall asleep, but you keep waking up at night. A tough sleep will leave you feeling exhausted and irritable the next day, either way.
Many who suffer from insomnia will frequently feel these emotions. A third of individuals in the UK are reported to have bouts of insomnia throughout their lives. While it can influence anyone at any age, it seems that individuals over the age of 60 and women are more vulnerable.

Different Types of Insomnia

There are several distinct forms of insomnia, but they are commonly grouped into two categories:
1. Temporary Insomnia

When it lasts between one night and three to four weeks, insomnia is known as transient or acute.
Jet lag, a shift of schedule or working environments, stress, caffeine, and alcohol are typical causes of transient insomnia.
Transient or sporadic insomnia is the name of certain examples of temporary insomnia. This is where the person occasionally develops sleeping difficulties over months or years.

2. Persistent Insomnia

This is considered chronic insomnia as well. The problem would usually continue almost nightly, for a period of four weeks. This may also occur as sleep is disturbed by pain or treatment from medical conditions. This may include arthritis, Parkinson's disease, asthma, allergies, chemicals that change, or concerns with mental health.

Symptoms Of Insomnia

Based on specific conditions, signs vary. There are common symptoms, however, including:

- keeping up at night for long hours.
- Not being conscious of falling asleep.
- Waking up during the night several times.
- Waking up very early and being unable to sleep again.
- Feeling exhausted the next morning and groggy.
- Finding it impossible to focus or work correctly.
- The sense of irritability.

Causes of Insomnia

The problem has multiple possible sources. In certain cases, sleeplessness may be caused by only one cause, while others may undergo a mixture of variables.
Any of insomnia's possible causes include:

Conditions in Physical Fitness

If you suffer from a health issue that causes you discomfort, you can find falling asleep difficult.
Likewise, if you have a disease, like asthma, that affects your breathing. It is assumed that sleep cycles can also be caused by hormone disorders and urinary conditions.
There is a risk your sleep will be disturbed by the medicine you are taking. Talk to the doctor if you suspect a health condition or think that your medicine can trigger a problem with your sleep.

• Mental Health Conditions

Sleeping issues may be created by such mental health conditions. An individual with extreme depression, for instance, is more likely to suffer from insomnia. When a person loses sleep, the depressed moods that come with depression may also be exacerbated.
Another disorder that is often associated with insomnia is anxiety. Anxiety may cause an entity to feel tense, worried, and exhausted. These emotions can find it difficult to fall asleep. When trying to sleep, the mind of the person will always run, feeling as though they cannot "switch off." Sleep can also be disrupted by the concern and the person may wake up in the night. The anxiety about not having enough sleep will turn into a vicious circle if this trend continues.

• Lifestyle

Sleeping behaviors may be affected by everyday activities and lifestyles. For starters, if you drink alcohol daily, you can find that during the night you wake up. Alcohol is a stimulant and even after taking a few drinks it can appear easy to fall asleep, it typically contributes to bad sleep overall.
Drugs and caffeine can similarly lead to issues with sleep. Any addiction to drugs is going to affect how you sleep, so it is important to seek help. It is advised that you minimize the consumption of caffeine if you suffer from insomnia.
Worked late into the night will find it impossible to turn off the brain. For your internal clock, shift work will create chaos and make sleeping tricky. It could be worth reassessing your hours if your job (or work-related stress) is affecting your insomnia.

The Way Insomnia Works

People with insomnia also say they are "insomniacs"; that is, genetically predisposed to insomnia.
There should be nothing farther from the facts. There is a dormant time in any living organism, so sleep is normal, so insomnia is unnatural.
Insomnia in general is caused by an intrinsic fear that may be about families, economic problems, questions of self-esteem, and numerous other anxieties. Every single client is different. However, we can figure out what is happening and fix the symptoms at a subconscious level by using hypnotherapy for Insomnia, bringing you back to a normal sleep cycle.
"Almost 30 percent of the population has a sort of sleeplessness. Anxiety almost always underpins insomnia, and this anxiety interrupts the normal rhythm of sleep. This fear is something persons with insomnia appear to ruminate on when going to sleep, which is what hypnotherapy targets with insomnia. This rumination produces elevated levels of anxiety and hence, within the insomniac, an elevated degree of alertness and therefore sleep eludes them. This anxiety is often so poor that the client might not be really conscious of it and thus assumes that there is little cause for the loss of sleep. Paul White, the insomnia specialist at the Surrey Institute of Clinical Hypnotherapy.

Treatment For Insomnia

There are different methods you might take when treating sleeping issues. In order to remove all physical triggers, it is necessary to first talk to the doctor. To help you sleep, your doctor can prescribe that you take medication. This may be an efficient therapy for certain persons, but it is necessary to try to figure out the root cause of the problem. Behavioral therapies and voice therapies are also suggested.

Another treatment choice which many people find successful is hypnotherapy. Insomnia hypnotherapy can resolve the possible triggers while helping you relax and go to sleep. For example, if the cause of your insomnia is anxiety or depression, sleep hypnosis can supplement your established therapy. It can then help to change the sleeping routine by solving these problems.

Alternatively, hypnotherapy for insomnia will work to break this habit if a habit causes your insomnia (such as alcohol).

As the suggestions made by hypnosis therapy allow your mind and body to relax and get the sleep you need the worry, discomfort, and fear that can prevent you from falling asleep fade away.

Ogunyemi Biodun

Hypnotherapy For Sleep

Although there may be an apparent reason for some sleeping issues, others will not. If you are unclear whether you are having trouble sleeping, hypnotherapy for insomnia may be beneficial. A hypnotherapist can reach into the subconscious using multiple methods to discover what could have caused the issue. A personalized therapy developed by the hypnotherapist will begin after the cause is identified.

The habits of sleep disturbances will become ingrained in the subconscious when suffering from insomnia for a long period of time. The aim of hypnosis for insomnia is to engage with it and propose constructive changes. These suggestions will aim to break the habits of negative thinking that trigger the problem.

Teaching you how to relax is an essential aspect of hypnotherapy for insomnia. Physical or emotional stress can make sleeping uncomfortable for certain individuals. To help relieve anxiety, a hypnotherapist can use relaxing methods, such as gradual muscle relaxation.

A hypnotherapist will also teach you self-hypnosis. It will help you create a schedule, as well as learn how to deal with the problem triggering the causes. Using hypnosis at home for insomnia will help you put into your daily life the techniques you have gained in the session room.

What Exactly Is Sleep Hypnosis?

If there was an easy and risk-free sleep aid that you might use daily, wouldn't it be a dream? Well, there is one, and it's called hypnosis of sleep! Hypnosis has been a well-known calming and implicit suggestion method for well over a century. The increasing use of this mystical self-improvement approach has been ignited by the use of sleep hypnosis for stopping cigarettes, treating chronic pain, curing insomnia, and more. Sleep hypnosis is used by certain individuals as a technique to make them fall asleep. Sleep hypnosis, in a nutshell, is a procedure that requires directed thought to lead a person into a state of relaxation.

This comfortable state could, in fact, make it easier to fall asleep. Several types of sleep hypnosis available can be downloaded to your phone or device, although it is not certain whether they are accurate or not. Read on for information about what it is, whether you are trying sleep hypnosis, and find other techniques that may be more effective when you want to get a decent night's sleep.

Sleep hypnosis is a session through which a hypnotherapist directs a participant by verbal gestures to cause calm and a trance that may be used to help you drift to sleep, either in person or by a video.

Hypnosis helps the recipient to actively "sleep" while still subconsciously aware. The ensuing trancelike state happens with the delta, theta, alpha states of lower-level brainwave activation where conscious activity subsides, and subconscious activity rises. It is also possible to use sleep hypnosis to bring the listener into deep and restorative sleep.

Sleep hypnosis requires listening to a hypnotherapist's auditory signals that are meant to draw you by the force of persuasion into a trance-like condition. Hypnotherapists use multiple techniques, such as concentrated concentration, control of symptoms, and directed visualization, to promote relief.

A person who is hypnotized can hear phrases like "relax," "deep," "easy," and let go." These words are supposed to encourage someone to drift off to sleep.

A hypnosis session for sleep includes:

Settling down: The receiver lies down and gets settled.

Letting go The listener is directed to place aside any doubts or concerns.

Induction: By relaxing the conscious mind and opening up the subconscious, it prepares the listener to go further into relaxation.

Breathing: This segment requires deliberate breathing that takes the recipient into equilibrium even more intensely.

The suggestion: This entails directed visualization that plants the intended outcome into the subconscious mind of the listener, the longest and final part of the hypnosis.

You may be curious whether wishful thinking is hypnosis or if it works. Fortunately, there is considerable research on the subject of sleep hypnosis.

Conclusion

What specifically makes it so difficult for a woman to lose weight. To start off with, it is not uncommon for women to be carrying more fat than men are, which could be as much as twelve kilograms (26lbs). This weighs down on her system and is causing the body to hold on tightly to fat stores and calories. In this case, the more weight you have to lose, the harder it may be to lose.

Another fact that adds to the difficulty of women losing weight is that they're simply not as active as men are. It is unreasonable for a woman to expect herself to burn off fat by exercising too much. Yes, she needs to exercise every day, but she should make sure she doesn't overdo it.

It could be beneficial if your wife or girlfriend took up a plan such as gastric band hypnosis rapid weight loss. This will allow her diet plan and exercise program to be holistic in the sense that it deals with not only what she eats but also how much and how often she exercises. This will put the best possible weight loss plan into play and will make it easier for her to drop pounds.

As with all diet programs, there are certain restrictions that need to be adhered to in order for them to be effective. For instance, a woman needs to have a low-calorie diet that ensures she is consuming about 700 calories daily (or about 1,800 calories per day). It is also wise for her to exercise regularly but not excessively; she should aim for no more than two hours of exercise on any given day.

Waiting too long on the diet side of things will only result in a short-term weight loss plan and may even cause some adverse health effects. These range from feeling weak to low energy levels to even depression. It is crucial for a woman not to overdo the exercise side of things as well, especially if it means she's exercising while hungry.

The benefits of gastric band hypnosis rapid weight loss are numerous. There's the obvious fact that this will allow your wife or girlfriend to drop weight without much trouble, but there are other benefits as well, such as the fact that this program is holistic in nature and can help her with diet and exercise.

In addition, there are also health benefits that come along with this plan. Unlike certain other diet programs, gastric band hypnosis rapid weight loss does not have any adverse health effects. Although some side effects should be reported, such as dry mouth, they're not as dangerous as other health problems that may result from using other programs.

Finally, the cost-benefit of it, is also significant. It is very affordable, and the overall costs will go down if your wife or girlfriend decides to use it in combination with a gym membership. All in all, gastric band hypnosis rapid weight loss is a great option to help your wife or girlfriend lose weight and keep it off.

www.ingramcontent.com/pod-product-compliance
Lightning Source LLC
Chambersburg PA
CBHW060940050726
47592CB00003B/1040